DISCIPLINING HERMENEUTICS

Disciplining Hermeneutics

Interpretation in Christian Perspective

Edited by

Roger Lundin

WILLIAM B. EERDMANS PUBLISHING COMPANY
GRAND RAPIDS, MICHIGAN

 APOLLOS
LEICESTER, ENGLAND

© 1997 Wm. B. Eerdmans Publishing Co.

Published jointly in 1997 in the United States by Wm. B. Eerdmans Publishing Co.
255 Jefferson Ave. S.E., Grand Rapids, Michigan 49503
and in the UK by APOLLOS (an imprint of Inter-Varsity Press)
38 De Montfort Street, Leicester LE1 7GP, England

Typeset and printed in the United States of America

02 01 00 99 98 97   7 6 5 4 3 2 1

Library of Congress Cataloging-in-Publication Data

Disciplining hermeneutics : interpretation in Christian perspective /
edited by Roger Lundin.
p.   cm.
Includes bibliographical references.
ISBN 0-8028-0858-1 (pbk. : alk. paper)
1. Bible — Hermeneutics. I. Lundin, Roger.
BS476.D57   1997
220.6'01 — dc21   97-4925
CIP

British Library Cataloguing in Publication Data

A catalogue record for this book is
available from the British Library

ISBN 0-85111-453-9

Contents

The Speech of God:
Hermeneutics and the Word

The Truth of the Matter:
Interpretation as Art and Science

From Suspicion to Retrieval:
Hermeneutics and the Human Sciences

Revelation and Human Understanding:
General and Special Hermeneutics

Acknowledgments

Many people assisted in the writing and editing of this book. First, I would like to thank each of the nine scholars whose essays grace these pages. They wrote lively and engaging papers, responded promptly and graciously to my editorial suggestions and inquiries, and offered frequent encouragement to me throughout the process of editing. I owe a special debt to Kevin Vanhoozer, who suggested the title for this volume.

Before these essays were ever written, a great deal of planning went into the conference that served as the source of this book. That conference, "Hermeneutics and a Christian Worldview," was held at Wheaton College, November 17-18, 1994. It was made possible through a generous grant from the Institute for Advanced Christian Studies; without that grant, neither the conference nor this book would have been possible. In planning the conference, I worked with colleagues Jim Mathisen, Tim Phillips, and Jay Wood. I thank each of them for their excellent contributions to the project; Tim Phillips was especially helpful in orchestrating the complex logistical arrangements of the conference.

My preliminary work on this project began when I was on academic leave to do research for another book, a biography of Emily Dickinson. That leave was made possible through a fellowship from the Pew Evangelical Scholarship Initiative. I am grateful to the Pew Charitable Trusts for its support.

I completed my final editing of the manuscript while also working on another project on hermeneutics supported by the Calvin Center for

Christian Scholarship. For their generous sponsorship of Christian scholarship, I wish to thank Calvin College and the governing board of the Calvin Center.

In the final stages of this project, two student assistants, Tim Lindgren and Matt Lundin, put in long hours tracking down references and verifying citations. They did their work thoroughly and with good cheer and thus made my own final editing much easier than it might otherwise have been.

This book is dedicated to Arthur Holmes, Professor of Philosophy Emeritus at Wheaton College. For half a century Arthur has faithfully and brilliantly served the Kingdom of God as a teacher, scholar, and mentor. He had the original idea for the conference and helped to secure funding to support the entire project. For some of us who have contributed to this volume, Arthur has been a teacher; for others of us, he has been a disciplinary or institutional colleague and friend; for all of us, he stands as a splendid example of how to serve God in the life of the mind with diligence, charity, and integrity.

ROGER LUNDIN

Introduction

ROGER LUNDIN

"A physicist friend of mine once said that in facing death, he drew some consolation from the reflection that he would never again have to look up the word 'hermeneutics' in the dictionary," wrote Nobel Prize–winning physicist Steven Weinberg in an essay not long ago, no doubt giving voice to the fears and frustrations that many feel when they hear the word.[1] To many who have become familiar with hermeneutics through debates in the church and the academy, it may appear to be a subject that is at one and the same time absolutely vital, irremediably controversial, and utterly incomprehensible.

To a significant extent, our uncertainty about hermeneutics may be due to the widely varying claims that contemporary scholarship makes about interpretation. We are told that the study of hermeneutics involves a never-ending task of assessment and reassessment. It demands of us an arduous reflection upon the art of human understanding and textual interpretation. Within the Christian church, an air of crisis seems to hover over discussions of hermeneutics. We hear of dire threats to the stability of meaning and of the pressing need to defend specific views of the inspiration and interpretation of the Scriptures. And in the larger culture, as in the church, disputes about interpretation attract widespread attention and arouse considerable anxiety. Stephen Weinberg's essay, for instance, deals

---

1. Steven Weinberg, "Sokal's Hoax," *The New York Review of Books* 42, no. 13 (8 Aug. 1996): 11.

1

with one of the most celebrated academic hoaxes in recent years: the un-witting publication of a parody by a journal dealing in the theory of inter-pretation. Entitled "Transgressing the Boundaries: Toward a Transformative Hermeneutics of Quantum Gravity," the article claimed that the mathe-matical constants of physics are nothing more than interpretive constructs. It is a measure of the confusion about hermeneutics today that the editors of the journal took the author, physicist Alan Sokal, to be serious, when he was merely enjoying a hearty laugh at their expense.

Yet even as many authorities urge us to ponder the complexity of the hermeneutical task, others encourage us to consider interpretation an act as natural to human life as the act of breathing. Each of us is at every moment an interpreter. Whether negotiating our way through the signs and signals at a clogged intersection, following the to-and-fro of an exciting basketball game, or quietly reading a Pauline epistle, we are engaged in hermeneutical practice. And it appears that we engage in such practice effortlessly and without reflection.

But if we are all interpreters just by the mere right of birth, then why all the fear and fuss about hermeneutics? Why, one might legitimately wonder, ought we to bother with the study of a practice that is natural, universal, and utterly unavoidable? Or, conversely, if the confusion about hermeneutics is as great as some allege, how is one to make sense of so many conflicting claims?

The essays in this volume speak directly to such questions. They do so out of a conviction that sustained reflection on hermeneutics may deepen the Christian mind and discipline Christian interpretive practice. Through a focus upon specific interpretive controversies, the authors in this book account for the present interest in hermeneutics and suggest lines of reso-lution for pressing disputes. Each essay was originally written for a confer-ence on "Hermeneutics and a Christian Worldview" at Wheaton College and then rewritten for publication in this book. Each of the four major essays from across the disciplines — by Nicholas Wolterstorff (philosophy), Donald Marshall (English), David Lyon (sociology), and Kevin Vanhoozer (theology) — is followed by responses that engage them on central issues of contention.

With its format of assertion and response, this book lays out many of the main possibilities for Christian hermeneutical thought and practice today. The disagreements among authors should alert us to important theological differences and point us to areas where Christian scholars need to engage in further research and debate. But at the same time, the many points of convergence and agreement to be found among these authors might encourage a church beset by claims of interpretive crisis. For all of their differences, the nine authors in this volume share a remarkable number of beliefs about the nature of interpretation and the tasks facing the Christian scholar in the postmodern world.

Divine Discourse and the Origins of Hermeneutics

In the opening essay of the book, Nicholas Wolterstorff analyzes the paradox at the heart of contemporary hermeneutics. "Interpretation does not have to be agonized; usually it is not," he observes. "Its results do not have to be seriously contested; most of them are not." Through much of our daily lives, we go about the business of interpreting without difficulty or care. But it is also the case, Wolterstorff acknowledges, that we live at a time of deepening hermeneutical crisis. "Hermeneutics arose not out of pure intellectual wonder but out of a crisis in interpretative practice" in the eighteenth and nineteenth centuries, says Wolterstorff. Furthermore, "the crisis in the practice of biblical interpretation . . . has not only continued but deepened and spread, so that the practices used for interpreting a vast array of other texts are now similarly in crisis." For all the ease that we experience in reading the signs, gestures, and symbols that we encounter every day, the interpretation of ancient and authoritative texts has become problematic in modernity. Or to put it another way, hermeneutics involves the study of a natural practice that has come upon a set of unnatural difficulties.

Wolterstorff's point about the naturalness of interpretation echoes a cardinal tenet of twentieth-century hermeneutical theory. It is that textual interpretation is but one form of the universal art of human understanding. In the words of Hans-Georg Gadamer, understanding is neither a unique act nor an occasional phenomenon. It "is not a resigned ideal of human experience," nor is it a rigorous philosophical ideal to be contrasted "to the naivete of unreflecting life." Instead, it is "the original characteristic of the being of human life itself," the universal and unavoidable characteristic of the human orientation to the world.[2]

2. Hans-Georg Gadamer, *Truth and Method,* 2nd rev. ed., trans. Joel Weinsheimer and Donald G. Marshall (New York: Crossroad, 1989), p. 259.

But if that is the case, we come back to the question implicit in Wolterstorff's claims about the modern hermeneutical crisis. If textual interpretation is one form of the universal art of human understanding, why has hermeneutics become so controversial in the modern world? In the landmark book of twentieth-century hermeneutical thought, *Being and Time*, Martin Heidegger argued that although our present crisis might be traced back to the ancient Greeks, its real sources lay closer to home. They could be found in the philosophical abstraction of René Descartes and the rationalism of the Enlightenment.[3] According to Heidegger, Gadamer, and Paul Ricoeur, among others, the Cartesian tradition called interpretation into question in a radical way and consigned hermeneutics to a decidedly secondary status. In Descartes's rationalist scheme, the act of securing knowledge was to proceed along strict procedural lines. For Descartes, before the mind began the search for truth, it had to dispose of all prejudices and assumptions. Interpretation could take place only after the unimpeded mind had secured the unadorned truth.

Heidegger and those who have followed him have countered the Cartesian denigration of hermeneutics by arguing that interpretation is built into the very structures that make human understanding of any kind possible. "When we have to do with anything," Heidegger asserts in *Being and Time*, "the mere seeing of the Things which are closest to us bears in itself the structure of interpretation. . . . An interpretation is never a presuppositionless apprehending of something presented to us."[4] In the Heideggerian tradition, our prejudices, or "prejudgements," do not impede the acquisition of knowledge but make it possible for us to understand anything at all. "Long before we understand ourselves through the process of self-examination, we understand ourselves in a self-evident way in the family, society, and state in which we live," Gadamer observes. *"That is why the prejudices of the individual, far more than his judgments, constitute the historical reality of his being."*[5] As Wolterstorff asserts, "interpretation does not have to be agonized," because it is a universal, natural phenomenon.

Like Heidegger and Gadamer, Wolterstorff suggests that in hermeneutics, it is modernity that has made the once natural seem unnatural. He

3. Martin Heidegger, *Being and Time*, trans. John Macquarrie and Edward Robinson (New York: Harper & Row, 1962).

4. Heidegger, *Being and Time*, ¶32.

5. Gadamer, *Truth and Method*, pp. 276-77.

traces the present crisis to two main sources: what he calls the historico-critical movement of the Enlightenment and the Romantic hermeneutics of Friedrich Schleiermacher. The historico-critical school first pruned away from the meaning of the Bible all assertions that might possibly contradict the assumptions about reality held by enlightened interpreters. "If you believe that miracles do not occur," Wolterstorff points out, you are left to hypothesize why biblical writers "would have used miracle stories to describe nonmiraculous events."

Of course, one might argue that the eighteenth- and nineteenth-century practices that Wolterstorff criticizes are simple variations upon the ancient practice of allegory. Throughout the history of interpretation, later generations have employed allegory to overcome the strangeness of ancient texts. With roots in Judaism, ancient Greece, and early and medieval Christianity, allegory had always involved the effort to make relevant texts or beliefs rendered obscure by historical change. In markedly different ways, Plato and the Greek tragedians employed allegory to interpret and sustain the Homeric myths; and in the early centuries of the Christian era, Philo and Origen attempted allegorical reconciliations of their respective Jewish and Christian beliefs with the main body of Greek philosophy.[6]

But it is not the practice of allegory that Wolterstorff criticizes. Instead, he questions the term "historico-critical," because he is struck by "how little there is of the historical, how much of the critical" in this modern approach to ancient texts. There arose in Western culture with and after Descartes a new and revolutionary assumption about the need for critical detachment in one's approach to texts and the truth. Whereas allegory belongs to the development of an ongoing tradition, the historico-critical approach to the Bible assumes a radical break in that tradition. The historico-critical approach has been shaped, Wolterstorff argues, almost entirely by the theological, epistemological, and historical assumptions of modernity. "Rather than being erected firmly on discoveries in the sands, the discipline strikes me, in good measure, as reflecting ourselves back to ourselves," he concludes.

Schleiermacher struck what Wolterstorff calls "a second massive blow . . . on the traditional practice of biblical interpretation." Fueled by his Romantic assumptions about language and the self, Schleiermacher con-

---

6. For a thorough examination of allegory and hermeneutics, see Gerald L. Bruns, *Hermeneutics Ancient and Modern* (New Haven: Yale Univ. Press, 1992), pp. 83-103.

sidered discourse to be a form of "self-expression in symbolic mode." With
Schleiermacher the goal of interpretation became the retrieval of an
author's intention; it followed logically that if writing is an act of self-
expression, then interpretation must entail the recovery of the intention
behind the expression.

But like the critical distancing called for in Cartesianism, the search
for intentions turns the natural act of understanding into an unnatural
form of interpretation. In Gadamer's words, Schleiermacher did not seek
"the unity of hermeneutics in the *unity of the content of tradition* to which
understanding is applied, but . . . in the unity of a procedure." We need
procedures and a universal hermeneutic to understand texts, whether they
are oral or written, because "the experience of the alien and the possibility
of misunderstanding is [sic] universal." With Schleiermacher, "in a new and
universal sense, alienation is inextricably given with the individuality of the
Thou."[7] Hermeneutics is the "art of avoiding misunderstanding," but it
must be practiced with the rigor of a science: "misunderstanding occurs as
a matter of course, and so understanding must be willed and sought at
every point."[8]

Schleiermacher argued that to understand a text "the interpreter
must put himself both objectively and subjectively in the position of the
author." The interpreter does so objectively through an exhaustive study
of the historical and linguistic background of the text. "The more we
learn about an author, the better equipped we are for interpretation," the
ultimate goal of which is "to understand the text at first as well as and
then even better than its author."[9]

In reacting against the psychologizing of interpretation in Schleiermacher's Romanticism, twentieth-century hermeneutical theorists have
moved to what Wolterstorff considers the other extreme, that of abandoning intention and seeking instead to capture the *sense of the text*. Rather
than seeing texts as ciphers that conceal the hidden intentions of their
authors, the structuralist reaction to Romanticism has dwelt almost exclusively on the verbal surface of texts. The *sense of the text*, in Wolterstorff's
words, is "the totality of [the] contextual senses of its constituent sentences."

7. Gadamer, *Truth and Method*, pp. 178-79.
8. "Hermeneutics: The Handwritten Manuscripts," in *Friedrich Schleiermacher:
Pioneer of Modern Theology*, ed. Keith W. Clements (London: Collins, 1987), p. 166.
9. "Hermeneutics: The Handwritten Manuscripts," p. 167.

Wolterstorff believes that we must "liberate ourselves from the grip of the notion that there is nothing between Romanticism and Structuralism." He suggests the alternative of attempting to discern "what the author did in fact say by authoring his text." His view is informed by the speech act theory of J. L. Austin and focuses upon the *illocutionary* action performed by an author in the act of writing; what, he asks, did an author accomplish through the writing of a work? To make this judgment, an interpreter will consider the intentions of an author and the *sense of the text*, with the goal in mind of discovering "what someone said" through the writing of a text.

Wolterstorff calls this form of understanding "authorial discourse interpretation" and sees in it a useful way of resolving conflicts that have plagued modern biblical interpretation. The Bible employs what he calls *double discourse,* speech in which one person says something by way of another person saying something. The speech of the scriptural writers was *deputized* speech. With a theory of *double discourse,* Wolterstorff argues, we can understand how "God can speak by way of the infirm and fallible speech of us human beings." In attending to what the biblical text actually says, we can discern the intentions of its human authors as well as the overall sense of the individual works and the biblical whole; further, by means of such close attention, we can also come to learn what God has meant to say through those whom he has deputized to speak on his behalf.

Although he criticizes Ricoeur on several counts in his essay, Wolterstorff resembles the French philosopher in his efforts to bring about a *rapprochement* between the continental and Anglo-American philosophical traditions. He employs analytic methods and deals with English philosophical sources to reach conclusions that converge at many points with the Heideggerian tradition in hermeneutics. Like Gadamer, Ricoeur, and others, Wolterstorff denies the possibility of arriving at a presuppositionless point of understanding for interpretation. (Reformed theology clearly plays a role in this and other aspects of Wolterstorff's view of interpretation.) His skepticism about Schleiermacher's view of discourse as self-expression and his confidence about recovering an author's intention also place Wolterstorff in the mainstream of contemporary hermeneutical theory.

Merold Westphal wittily notes that "by seeking a middle way between those with too weak a view and those with too strong a view of divine discourse, [Wolterstorff] pretty well guarantees that he will get shot at from both sides." Indeed, that proves to be the case with the responses to Wolterstorff's proposals by I. Howard Marshall, an English New Testament scholar, and Westphal, an American philosopher with strong interests in the continental tradition. Marshall cautions against speeding down the Continental road, while Westphal chides Wolterstorff for keeping his foot on the brake all the while.

At the heart of Marshall's concerns about *double discourse* is an evangelical Protestant apprehension about the place of tradition in the Christian faith. Gadamer and other contemporary hermeneutical theorists place a great emphasis upon the role tradition plays in grounding interpretation and establishing the truth. By doing so, it provides a useful counterweight to the neglect of the role of tradition and the church in evangelical Protestantism. Lacking a clearly developed theology of the Holy Spirit, that evangelical tradition has found it difficult to account for the divine role in what seem to be very human processes. In part, Wolterstorff's theory of *double discourse* is an attempt to make up for that lack by providing a way of understanding God's deputizing and appropriating of human speech.

A potential difficulty with this approach, Marshall points out, is that it transfers "the divine action, which is apparently one of passive approval, to after the speaking, instead of, as traditionally, being an action that somehow influences the speaker and does so before or during the speech." But if it is "obvious that not all human speech" is of a type that God can appropriate, how do we determine what is different about the speech that God does appropriate? And if God's *authorizing* of human speech occurs after the fact of that speech's utterance, what implications does this view have for our understanding of the biblical canon? As Marshall observes, the classic Protestant view has been that in forming the canon, the church recognized "the inherent authority" of the books it was canonizing and did not confer that authority on them.

If Marshall fears that Wolterstorff's theory of *double discourse* places too much faith in tradition and natural human agency, then Westphal worries that the theory does not take them seriously enough. He notes the similarities between Wolterstorff's account of interpretation and those offered by Heidegger and Gadamer. They differ on the mechanisms of construal: Gadamer thinks of interpretation as metaphorical ("seeing something as something"), while Wolterstorff focuses on its usefulness as a human action ("making something of something"). But Westphal argues that Gadamer and Wolterstorff agree that "the phenomenon that is construed . . . underdetermines its interpretation and does not dictate it." Neither authors nor texts can determine their own meaning.

Where Marshall questions Wolterstorff's strong reading of tradition and human agency, Westphal faults him for failing to embrace "the strong reason" for "rejecting the claim that the intent of the author is the meaning of the text." Relying heavily upon the analogies between the musical performance of a score and the reading of a text, Westphal argues that authors have no power to "dictate their own interpretation." He calls texts "virtual meanings" that await their actualization in "readings that will be performances."

Westphal's critique is rooted in theological convictions about the limits placed upon men and women by their sin and finitude. "Perhaps God does not need to interpret, but we do," he wryly observes. "It is part of our finitude." As he sees it, that finitude places radical constraints upon our ability to know things with certainty and requires us to engage in a constant reassessment — reinterpretation — of texts and reality. Our acts of understanding are always bound to be flawed efforts to get it right in our reading of books and things. "There is no such thing as *the* interpretation of a text," Westphal asserts. All that we can aim at is to produce one of that "plurality of differing interpretations" that eventually prove to be "deserving of high praise."

This sharp view of finitude also leads Westphal to minimize the differences that separate critics of Enlightenment objectivism from one another. In his account of contemporary hermeneutics, Enlightenment foundationalism is the common enemy of poststructuralists and fundamentalists alike, as well as of all who inhabit any middle ground between their extremes. Confident that the history of interpretive disputes will disclose which interpretations are "deserving of high praise" and which are worthy of censure or dismissal, Westphal does not share Wolterstorff's and Marshall's concern to establish limits to interpretive freedom. "While texts may well be too weak to determine their own interpretation single-handedly," he concludes, "they do have a rather remarkable recalcitrance in the presence of arbitrariness."

Between them, then, Wolterstorff, Marshall, and Westphal map out the major hermeneutical positions held by evangelical and Reformed Protestants today. Rooted in the presuppositionalism and common grace theology of Dutch Calvinism, Wolterstorff seeks to balance his critique of foundationalism with an appreciation of necessary interpretive constraints.

His theory of *double discourse* and the *authorizing* of Scripture is intended to give full play to the humanity of the biblical authors and the historicity of language use while it secures the act of reading against the possibilities of interpretive anarchy.

In contrast, I. Howard Marshall presses the concerns of a more avowedly evangelical understanding of Scripture and a more pointedly empirical view of the interpretive process. In his questioning of the idea of the *authorizing* of Scripture, his concerns with the sequencing of canonization, and his desire to press the matters of factual contents and historical referents, Marshall gives voice to the anxieties of a generation of conservative biblical scholars confronting the brave new world of postfoundational hermeneutics.

The world that puzzles and concerns Marshall is the same one that Westphal welcomes with delighted relief. He speaks for many contemporary Christian students of culture who yearn to see the church break free of its Enlightenment and fundamentalist bondage. For Westphal, there is little point in quibbling about the hair-splitting distinctions bequeathed to us by centuries of foundationalism. It would be better, he asserts, for us to drop our concern for interpretive certainty and get on with the hermeneutical tasks that fall to us inevitably as a consequence of our finitude.

Many Readings, One Truth

The discussion of biblical interpretation by Wolterstorff, Marshall, and Westphal establishes the groundwork for the remainder of the essays in the book. Donald Marshall, for example, develops further the debate that they have initiated about the relationship between the Christian faith's claims to truth and the common claim of contemporary hermeneutical theory that, in Westphal's words, "there is no such thing as *the* interpretation of a text." If all we can achieve in our reading of the Bible is *an* interpretation of the text, how are we to discover *the* truth revealed by the God who speaks through that Bible? Donald Marshall confronts the problem directly at the beginning of his essay: "I think a Christian has to ask this fundamental hermeneutic question: Can truth come to us through an interpretation?"

Marshall examines this question with the help of Aristotle and Gadamer. He maps out the paths that Aristotle suggested we might take to the truth, through "*episteme*, or certain knowledge based on reasoning from sound principles; *techne,* or knowledge shown in the construction of things; and *phronesis,* or knowledge shown in the choice of right actions."

Episteme is at the heart of the Cartesian search for indubitable epistemological foundations and as such has been the subject of substantial critique in the modern hermeneutical tradition. There is a good deal that we need to "concede to the claims of conceptual rationality," Marshall argues, for "conceptual presuppositions" undergird all attempts to convey meaning and understand texts. If we did not possess the frameworks constructed by the rationality of *episteme,* we would find it impossible to make intelligible sense of any utterance or text. But Marshall points out that it is also the case that "if truth is to come to us through interpretation, conceptual rationality cannot be what we are seeking." That is, if interpretation of a text brought us such rationally ordered knowledge, it would only be giving us what we had known before we began. In such a view, interpretation could only illustrate or confirm what we had already learned by other means.

Because it also subjects the objects of its study to predictive control, *techne* seems to Marshall no more satisfactory than *episteme* as a model for the discovery of truth through interpretation. To be sure, he credits *techne* with a great deal, and argues that a significant yield has come from this approach to knowledge. For example, Marshall focuses on the historical and critical studies that at the beginning of the modern era dramatically altered the Western view of ancient texts. Where Wolterstorff looks skeptically at the "historico-critico" method — "What impresses me . . . is how little there is of the historical, how much of the critical" — Marshall finds more to praise. To such study of ancient texts, he writes, "we also owe a vast body of information about the text of Scripture, the archaeology and history of the Near East, and the historical variety of religious ideas among the Jews."

On one level, then, *techne* has a high yield when applied to the study of texts. It turns the text into an object to be classified and studied with scientific precision and the rigor of historical method. Yet Marshall concludes that despite its achievements, modern "scientific knowledge is not what we are seeking in understanding Scripture or literary texts. In historical research on the truth of Scripture or the historical forces that produce a text, we lose sight of the real subject." That "real subject" of reading is the transformation of the interpreter's life.

Phronesis leads to wisdom and right action and is the form of knowledge that validates interpretation's claims to truth, according to Marshall. Its purpose is to "mediate between the particulars of our action and the principles that ground and justify them." What Marshall calls "the two great constructive powers of reason and modern science" perform the necessary task of distancing us critically from the object of our study or concern. *Phronesis* brings the dead object to life by allowing it to address us in our immediate situation. The wise interpreter grasps "a question — not a question we put critically to a text, but the question the text puts to us." In responding openly to the question a text puts to us, we testify or witness to "its truth through our own actions."

Marshall recognizes that in a Christian view of truth the particularity of *phronesis* must be taken up into a larger frame of reference. He believes that in Christian history, figural interpretation has been crucial in the effort to give the limited judgments of *phronesis* a universal scope. Figural interpretation, which dates back to the beginnings of the Christian church, involves seeing events, persons, and experiences as having been prefigured in earlier scriptural accounts. In this vision of interpretation, the past becomes prophecy and the present fulfillment. Thus, the New Testament fulfills the promise of the Old, just as the events unfolding in the history and the experiences of individual believers draw out the meaning in ancient stories and texts. To explain how figural interpretation completes and deepens the insights of *phronesis*, Marshall quotes Erich Auerbach, the literary historian who revolutionized the modern understanding of *figura:* "the history of no epoch ever has the practical self-sufficiency which, from the standpoint both of primitive man and of modern science, resides in the accomplished fact; all history, rather, remains open and questionable, points to something still concealed."[10]

At the end of his essay, Marshall answers his own opening question by asserting that truth comes to us through interpretation when individual interpretations of texts take their place in a much larger scheme of anticipation and fulfillment. "The claim to truth and hence to universality of the interpreter's answer to the text," he writes, lies "in the openness of action to a future where it will have consequences and serve as the material of further interpretation." In the final analysis, all acts of interpretation have an eschatological dimension in that they look forward to the kingdom of

10. Erich Auerbach, "Figura," in *Scenes From the Drama of European Literature* (New York: Meridian, 1959), p. 58.

God, when the "meaning of the whole of history [and all texts] will be revealed."

In many ways, Donald Marshall's treatment of *phronesis* resembles Merold Westphal's stress upon a "plurality of differing interpretations deserving of high praise." Both are eager to maintain the openness of the interpretive process and avoid the finality of scientific summation or rational categorization. Each also emphasizes the finite and situated nature of the interpreter and his or her interpretive judgments. In interpreting, they argue, we are limited by the fact that we are always responding to something already posited and must give our own efforts up to the future; just as texts cannot determine the reading that we will give to them, neither can we control the future course of our own interpretive acts.

In a superb book on contemporary hermeneutics, Joel Weinsheimer suggests that problems of the kind that Marshall and Westphal face are inherent in the hermeneutical situation. "An interpretation as such is different from and yet also the same as what it interprets," Weinsheimer writes. If it is not in some sense the same as what it interprets, "it is not an interpretation but a new text, unrelated to the first; and if it is not (in some sense) different, it is not an interpretation of the text but a copy of it." As a result, all sound interpretive practice involves movement between two poles, that of correctness and that of creativity. "Interpretations are necessarily *of* the text," which "explains why there can be wrong interpretations." On the other hand, texts invite "interpretations that are not just duplicates of it but genuinely other." Weinsheimer concludes that "if the text had but one right interpretation and many wrong ones, or many right interpretations and no wrong one, there would not be a problem."[11] But that, we know, is not the case.

There is a decidedly Barthian air to Westphal's emphasis upon finitude and Marshall's stress upon the eschatological nature of truth; their views of interpretation and truth assume a dramatic gap separating earth from heaven and provisional judgment from certain truth. In her essay, Ellen Charry wonders about this gap. She questions Marshall's sharp distinction "between *techne* and *phronesis,* between skill and wisdom, or as he treats them, science and art." She is concerned that in "backing off from claiming that Christian interpretation is a science" and thinking of it instead as an "act of conceptual clarification," Marshall may concede too much to the

11. Joel Weinsheimer, *Philosophical Hermeneutics and Literary Theory* (New Haven: Yale Univ. Press, 1991), p. 87.

epistemological spirit of the age. Theological and moral reasoning, she says, must and can "lay claim to a stronger basis than that which comes from standing within a community of interpreters only."

In contrast to Marshall's Gadamerian stress on *phronesis*, Charry promotes what she terms "a cautious critical theological realism." She does so by elaborating a series of analogies between medical practice and Christian proclamation. As medical science can claim to be true because of its predictive and curative powers, so too may Christian reasoning "lay claim to truth because it produces results." Her argument is that as important as wisdom and narrative coherence may be in guiding us to the good life, they must be subordinated in some sense to the "general propositions" at the core of the Christian faith. Christian doctrine can and must provide standards for Christian interpretation, just as scientific research sets the standards for the practice of medicine, for "there is more at work in Christian interpretation than conceptual clarity. There is also the bedrock of Christian doctrine to which interpretation is called back."

Charry's critique of Marshall raises again the question of what ought to regulate interpretive practice. Those who work in the tradition of Heidegger and Gadamer appear relatively comfortable with what might be called a form of "hermeneutical traditionalism." In this view, truth is both passed on through tradition and developed through interpretation and dispute. The truth is that which emerges gradually in the history of interpretive practice and which awaits its full revelation in the eschaton. Following the lead of Gadamer and others, Christian theorists who work in this tradition are more interested in describing interpretive practices than in prescribing interpretive standards.

Those, on the other hand, who stand at a critical distance from the tradition of Heidegger are more likely to seek to secure and defend a foundational set of doctrinal assertions and epistemological assumptions. They worry that a too great emphasis upon truth as that which emerges in Christian interpretive practice may neglect the understanding of truth as that which establishes right practices. The theological critics of the Heideggerian tradition argue that a commitment to truth requires a vigilant concern for the role of factual references and confessional beliefs in our interpretation of sacred texts in particular. "Was there a 'Jesus' who is the historical referent of the stories" of the Gospels, asks Marshall, "and are the stories themselves correctly recorded?" With questions such as these, the cautious realists continue to test the claims of contemporary hermeneutical theory.

Breaking Boundaries:
Hermeneutics and the Human Sciences

In focusing upon the specific issues of truth and scriptural interpretation, the chapters in the first half of this book point to the unmistakable origins of modern hermeneutics in the confessional beliefs and interpretive practices of the Christian church. With David Lyon's essay, we come upon the modern expansion of hermeneutics far beyond its theological origins and historic boundaries. At the end of the eighteenth century, the Kantian revolution in epistemology granted sweeping new powers to perception, and by implication, to interpretation. In doing so, it dramatically expanded the scope of modern hermeneutical reflection. No longer solely the domain of the church, hermeneutics was transformed into a general science of interpretation and human understanding, and with that transformation, the modern social sciences were born.

This expansion of hermeneutics had a number of unintended consequences, which Lyon succinctly summarizes at the start of his essay. "What happened in biblical hermeneutics?" he asks. "What began as a science of interpretation, for better understanding the text, has often ended as a pretext for doubting or even discarding the text." Lyon notes that the relativism and cynicism of contemporary interpretation theory may have their origins, ironically enough, in the Reformation's interpretive practices. Relativism is rooted, in part, in the Reformation's "swing toward private interpretation," and the hermeneutics of suspicion can be traced to the desacralizing impulse behind the Protestant critique of the Mass and the Catholic sacraments.

Lyon argues that by opening "doors for dialogue," postmodernism may afford the Christian church the opportunity to "resist relativism" and retrieve "the ontological foundations of communal being-in-the-world." But according to Lyon, before "retrieval" can begin, the church must acknowledge the critique of "the hermeneutics of suspicion." This is the name given by Ricoeur to interpretive practices that arose in Europe at the end of the nineteenth century. The great modern "masters of suspicion" — Friedrich Nietzsche, Karl Marx, and Sigmund Freud — looked "upon the whole of consciousness primarily as 'false' consciousness" and carried the Cartesian stance of doubt "to the very heart of the Cartesian stronghold," human consciousness. Descartes had assumed that "in consciousness, meaning and consciousness of meaning coincide," writes Ricoeur. "Since

Marx, Nietzsche, and Freud, this too has become doubtful. After the doubt about things, we have started to doubt consciousness."[12] Lyon believes that the hermeneutics of suspicion has had the beneficial effect of dethroning Enlightenment rationality, discrediting the myth of inevitable progress through social engineering, and dismantling patriarchy and colonialism.

The fact that a sociologist writes as enthusiastically as David Lyon does about hermeneutics demonstrates the extraordinary growth of a discipline once associated exclusively with the study of biblical texts. In philosophy, the work of Kant and Hegel paved the way for the expansion of hermeneutics by revolutionizing Western ideas of the mind's constitutive powers. In actual interpretive practice, the changes began several hundred years ago with the historical-critical method. The critical study of the Bible was spurred by a number of forces, almost all of which were associated with the growth of rationalism and the rise of the scientific method. First, the ordered world of Cartesian and Newtonian mechanism served to make the miraculous, dynamic world of the Scriptures seem distant and alien; then the same philosophical approach and scientific method that had fostered the gap between the modern world and the ancient texts was called upon to close it.

The historical-critical study of the Scriptures involved a distancing that turned the biblical text into an alien collection of signs needing to be deciphered. From that point on, it was inevitable that the practices used in the critical treatment of ancient texts would be extended to the study of all forms of human language use and symbolic behavior. As Willie Jennings writes, "on the way from Kant to Derrida, from Schleiermacher to Baudrillard, hermeneutics has been repositioned. Hermeneutics is now positioned as fully the *power* of reading."

Jennings shares Lyon's view of postmodernity "as an unsafe but creative theological space" but is less sanguine than Lyon about the immediate prospects of Christian dialogue with the postmodern temper. He depicts the postmodern world as an intersection where "information hyper-dissemination, cultural production and reproduction, and aggressive consumerism" collide and move on at dizzying speeds. "Standing at this intersection," Jennings observes, "modern Western people only hear a word of truth as an agreed-upon deception, a *policed* relativism."

12. Paul Ricoeur, *Freud and Philosophy: An Essay on Interpretation,* trans. Denis Savage (New Haven: Yale Univ. Press, 1970), p. 33.

Looming in the background of this definition of the postmodern view of truth as "agreed-upon deception, a *policed* relativism" is one of the great progenitors of the postmodern world, Nietzsche. In a well-known essay from 1873, the German philosopher argued that the human intellect is a powerful agent of "simulation" and that "only through forgetfulness can man ever achieve the illusion of possessing a 'truth.'" The truth, he asserted, is merely a "mobile army of metaphors, metonyms, and anthropomorphisms — in short, a sum of human relations, which have been enhanced, transposed, and embellished poetically and rhetorically. . . . Truths are illusions about which one has forgotten that this is what they are."[13] Given this profoundly disenchanted view of knowledge at the heart of postmodernity, Jennings asks, "can it [sociology] deliver on the historic promise of its discipline: objective vision (i.e., truth) of the social, without being destroyed by the hermeneutics of suspicion or dismissed by a policing relativism?"

To counter the corrosive effects of this relativism, Jennings proposes what he calls a "transformation of sociology: sociology must be reinvented as a theological and ethical discourse upon the social." If this transformation is to take place, "theology (and by implication the church) must reassert truth without seeking its reestablishment." Theology must go about this task by challenging postmodern claims that truth is an illusion and reality an unreality. Regardless of what postmodern theories of language may assert about reality, Jennings points out that morally sensible people awake each morning to discover that "a real world, real social conditions, real human beings are positioned before them, standing in real need and calling for care and concern." In response to this undeniable reality, Jennings calls for a "retrieval" of the truth that "involves remembering the care spoken of in the Jewish and Christian Scriptures, connecting it with the ontological situation of communal being-in-the-world, and using this hermeneutically to interpret contemporary social situations and processes."

Perhaps not surprisingly, the differences between Lyon and Jennings on postmodernity bring us back to points of disagreement among the other authors in this volume. In whatever form they surface, these disagreements have to do with the question of what to make of the postmodern moment. Should we welcome postmodern hermeneutical liberty because, to use a metaphor frequently employed, it creates a level playing field on which

---

13. Friedrich Nietzsche, "On Truth and Lie in the Extra-Moral Sense," in *The Portable Nietzsche*, ed. and trans. Walter Kaufman (New York: Penguin, 1968), pp. 46-47.

Christians are once again free to join the cultural fray? Lyon believes that we ought to accept the challenge and risk of this game: "The postmodern offers the opportunity not only to deny purpose but also to affirm it in new — or revived — neoprovidential ways." He admits that there is a palpable risk for Christian proclamation in the interpretive game as it is played under postmodern rules, "but the bigger risk is that a Christian perspective . . . would disappear by default. There is no risk-free space." Or ought we to look with skepticism upon that postmodern freedom and the game it invites us to play? Jennings believes that we should. He would have the church bear witness to revealed truth through its own theological discourse and through its merciful remembrance of "the care spoken of in the Jewish and Christian Scriptures."

Revelation and Reading

In his wide-ranging essay on modern hermeneutics, Kevin Vanhoozer develops an extended argument along the lines sketched out by Willie Jennings. And in doing so, Vanhoozer brings our attention back to the dominant role played by the Bible and biblical interpretation in all Christian reflection upon hermeneutics. Decidedly skeptical about the possibilities of postmodern theory in general, and of deconstruction in particular, Vanhoozer presses the case for theology to reclaim its rightful position in contemporary hermeneutical theory and practice. "The Bible should be read like any other book," he writes, but in turn, "every other book should be read like the Bible, from within a Christian worldview."

Vanhoozer argues that any theory or practice of interpretation is "theological" if it assumes that something " 'transcends' the play of language in writing." He calls the champions of deconstruction, such as Jacques Derrida and Roland Barthes, "countertheologians" because of their avowed refusal to believe in anything beyond the play of writing. In Vanhoozer's account, deconstruction and the larger crisis in contemporary literary theory originated in Nietzsche's announcement of the "death of God." The nineteenth-century disappearance of God as the author of meaning in history and nature has been followed by the twentieth-century disappearance of the human author. With all interpretive truth claims "dissolved in a [postmodern] sea of indeterminacy," he says, "hermeneutics has become the prodigal discipline, rejecting both the authority of the Father and the rationality of the Logos, squandering its heritage in riotous and rebellious reading."

As an alternative to what he terms "the interpretive violence" wreaked upon the text by deconstruction, Vanhoozer calls for a "hermeneutics of humility," which is "willing to receive something from the other, from the text, and from other interpreters." He advocates a form of hermeneutical confessionalism that does not so much declare, "Here I stand," as it asks instead, "How does it look where you stand?" Claiming Karl Barth and Paul Ricoeur as guides, Vanhoozer promotes an interpretive approach which grants that although our knowledge may not be absolute, it is sufficient to equip us to respond to the word of God. Like Barth and Ricoeur, he says that with "humble conviction" the Christian church should challenge our era to "read any other book like the Bible." We are to issue this challenge with the quiet confidence that "understanding is theological because we are only enabled to follow the issue of the text by the Holy Spirit."

Dallas Willard does not take issue with Vanhoozer's sharp critique of deconstruction but raises questions instead about the role assigned by him to the Holy Spirit in interpretation. He labels Vanhoozer's view of the Spirit's role as a case of "hermeneutical occasionalism." In calling it such, Willard has in mind the mind/body problem in the Cartesian tradition. With Descartes having declared the mind and body to be distinctly different essences, it fell to his intellectual descendants to explain how they interacted; Nicholas Malebranche thought that they did so when God took the occasion to cause what happened in one sphere to impinge upon the other.

In like manner, Willard suggests, Vanhoozer's view of the work of the Holy Spirit in interpretation is an attempt to account for the bridging of the gap between our finite, biased perspectives and "the (or a) *right* interpretation" of a text. Vanhoozer asserts both that "language does not bar us from reality" and that "reality comes mediated by language." According to Willard, "the problem is, how do we spell out this latter clause in such a way that the former *can* be true? How do we have *mediation* without *modification?*" Further, Willard argues, if in Vanhoozer's "clauses we replace the word *language* with the word *experience* or *consciousness* or even *thought,* we find our location in the problematic of modern thought, persisting ever since Descartes 'discovered' consciousness. Once you 'discover' it you get out only by a miracle."

Vanhoozer might respond that we need not have *"mediation* without *modification"* and that we cannot "replace the word *language* with the word *experience* or *consciousness* or even *thought.*" One of the central tenets of hermeneutical theory since Heidegger is that language is profoundly different from consciousness. It is neither necessary nor possible for us to "get out" of language, because language opens to us the world and the possibility of understanding. In the Heideggerian tradition, language is not the "prison house" described by Frederic Jameson in a book on contemporary literary theory.[14] Instead, as Gadamer eloquently states it, we ought to consider that "experience is not wordless to begin with, subsequently becoming an object of reflection by being named. . . . Rather, experience of itself seeks and finds words that express it." In doing so, we testify however unwittingly to our awareness that "the verbal world in which we live is not a barrier that prevents knowledge of being-in-itself but fundamentally embraces everything in which our insight can be enlarged and deepened."[15] And there is, after all, ample Christian warrant for such a high view of language, for "in the beginning was the Word, and the Word was with God, and the Word was God."

Conclusion

Since the essays in this volume had their origins in a conference setting, it is not surprising that they frequently highlight the differences separating Christian scholars on interpretive matters. The disciplinary and denominational distinctions among these authors are real and substantial. Social scientists are in the main more content than are theologians with the radical nature of postmodern critique, and philosophers steeped in continental philosophy may inevitably feel more at home in the world of Heidegger and Gadamer than do those whose primary commitments lie with the Anglo-American analytic tradition. Similarly, a view of interpretation rooted in the Calvinism of the Dutch Reformed Church will draw out different emphases than one that has emerged from mainstream American evangelicalism.

Whatever their differences, however, the authors of these essays demonstrate an impressive degree of unity on crucial hermeneutical points. For

14. Frederic Jameson, *The Prison-House of Language: A Critical Account of Structuralism and Russian Formalism* (Princeton: Princeton Univ. Press, 1972).

15. Gadamer, *Truth and Method,* pp. 417, 447.

example, all of them acknowledge that both texts and their interpreters are inescapably situated in their distinctive historical contexts and linguistic worlds. One will find nowhere in these pages the yearning to be free of history that marks some evangelical Christian hermeneutical theories. The authors in this book have no desire to neglect the traditions of the church, nor do they feel a need to obliterate the distance between us and the ancient texts that we struggle to understand. Not one of these authors would share the conviction of E. D. Hirsch — a belief widely held among conservative biblical scholars — that the goal of textual interpretation is the recovery of the intention of the text's author.[16] Such a view implies that it is possible for interpreters to set aside fully their own assumptions and understandings. The authors in this volume do not think that is possible. To one degree or another, each accepts as a given Gadamer's model of interpretation as a fusion of horizons.

While taking the situated nature of discourse and interpretation with utmost seriousness, the essayists in this volume also share a passion for truth and a belief in our ability to overcome illusions and know reality. They may not accept the naive Romantic intentionalism of Hirsch, but neither do they embrace its postmodern opposite of verbal freeplay. To be sure, they disagree on the extent to which the Christian interpreter should accept the epistemological revolution of postmodernity, but they agree on the need for a basic realism to undergird our interpretive endeavors.

That is to say that even as they engage the most challenging contemporary issues and literature on interpretive theory, the authors in this volume do so in the context of a clear affirmation of Christian faith. With the saints and simple believers of the ages, these scholars from across the disciplines work on vexing hermeneutical issues with the full confidence that God has created the world out of love and that he may be known through his revelation in the Scriptures, in human experience and the natural world, and in the person of Jesus Christ. They are driven, as we should be, to try to understand how it is that we interpret others, the world around us, and the Word of God. In their insightful handling of complex interpretive issues, the authors in this book seek to negotiate the narrow straits between absolute certainty and interpretive license. And as they chart the turbulent waters of the postmodern world, they may serve as savvy guides to assist us in our difficult passage to the truth.

16. See E. D. Hirsch Jr., *Validity in Interpretation* (New Haven: Yale Univ. Press, 1967).

The Speech of God:
Hermeneutics and the Word

The Importance of Hermeneutics
for a Christian Worldview

NICHOLAS WOLTERSTORFF

Hermeneutics is theory of interpretation. And what is interpretation? We speak of a musician's interpretation of a sonata, of a scientist's interpretation of the results of an experiment, of a literary critic's interpretation of a text, of a wife's interpretation of her husband's nervous behavior, of a physician's interpretation of a patient's symptoms, of the interpretation that a pair of students put on the fact that one of them received an A on a paper and the other a C when it was the very same paper but graded by two different instructors. Evidently interpretation is pervasive in human life.

Or maybe not. To conclude, on the basis of the observations I have just made, that interpretation is pervasive in human life requires assuming that the word *interpretation* picks out the same activity and result thereof in all of those cases — to assume that I was not using the word ambiguously. But I do myself regard that assumption as correct. It is fairly easy to say, in a rough and ready way, what that activity and result thereof is — though to move beyond a rough and ready statement to a refined and fully qualified statement would not be at all easy.

Each case involves the issue of what the person is *to make of* a certain phenomenon: what the scientist is to make of the experimental results, what the wife is to make of her husband's nervous behavior, and so forth. Each must determine what to make of it for the purpose of performing an activity of a certain sort on that phenomenon, or for the purpose of arriving at a certain sort of knowledge about it. The phenomenon in question does not automatically produce action or knowledge of that sort. The pianist wants to arrive at the point of performing a sonic realization of the sonata; to achieve that purpose, she has to figure out exactly what to make of the specifications of pitches, rhythms, and rests. She finds herself at the point of confronting alternative possibilities; so she has to interpret. The physician wants to arrive at the point of knowing what disease it is of which the patient's symptoms are a manifestation; to achieve that purpose, he has to figure out what to make of the patient's cough, what significance to attach to her aches and pains. He finds himself at the point of confronting alternative possibilities; so he has to interpret.

In general, we find ourselves with experience or perception of a certain phenomenon; we desire to do something of a certain sort with that phenomenon or to come to know something about it of a certain sort. To get from here to there we have to figure out what to make of what we presently experience or perceive of the phenomenon. With an eye on the sort of activity that we want to perform or the sort of knowledge that we want to acquire, we have to figure out what this phenomenon *means* or what *significance* to give it. Interpretation is that activity whereby we traverse that open space of alternative possibilities.

The expression "figuring out" suggests deliberation. This suggestion is misleading, however, for an act of interpretation can occur anywhere on the continuum from thoroughly habitual to agonizingly deliberative. The so-called hermeneutic tradition, at least when discussing interpretation of texts, has tended to focus its attention on that extreme end of the continuum where we find agonized deliberation. That tells us more about the mentality of characteristic members of the hermeneutic tradition than it does about the nature of interpretation. Interpretation does not have to be agonized; usually it is not. Its results do not have to be seriously contested; most of them are not. It is just that the agonized and contested cases draw attention to themselves more than the others do.

So, yes, interpretation is pervasive in human life. That reveals something deep and important about the sort of creatures we human beings are and about our place in creation. Our experience and perception of the items of reality leave open what we are to make of those items, as thus experienced and perceived, for many of the actions that we want to perform on them and for many of the things that we want to know about them.

But it does not follow that *hermeneutics* is important. Interpretation, yes. Interpretation is not only pervasive but unavoidable: without interpretation, we human beings could not live in this world of ours, given how we experience it. We are consigned to be, or honored with being, interpreting creatures. But *theory* of interpretation is a different matter. Why is hermeneutics important? Or is it?

I might begin to answer these questions by noting that if hermeneutics is important, it is certainly not *all important*. Most of us do most of our interpreting, and some of us do all of our interpreting, without having any *theory* of interpretation in hand. Mainly we are inducted by our fellow human beings into the already ongoing social practices of interpretation; here and there, upon experiencing where those practices work and where they do not, we learn to revise them and to institute new ones. But for the most part we do this without making use of *theories* of interpretation. Put the other way around: the very activities of devising and appropriating theories of interpretation presuppose the ability, on the part of the devisers and appropriators, to interpret.

In principle, theorizing about interpretation might have arisen out of the purely intellectual desire to understand this part of our human condition; and those who continue to engage in it might in principle do so for no other reason than to obtain the delight that comes with understanding. Naturally something has to pique one's curiosity; something has to lead one to steer one's mind in this direction. Sometimes we human beings do experience delight in coming to understand, just as we sometimes experience aesthetic delight; and the prospect of that delight sometimes motivates us. Maybe what we come to understand will also enable us to do something better: bake bread, act charitably, or gain power. But that does not take away from the fact that some of us sometimes just get delight in learning about, say, the nesting habits of penguins in the Antarctic.

But that is not how hermeneutics arose. If we adopt the standard view that Schleiermacher was the first who self-consciously engaged in theorizing about interpretation, then it is obvious that what first generated theorizing about interpretation was a perceived crisis in a certain practice of interpretation; namely, in the practice of interpreting the Christian Bible.[1] And

---

1. Friedrich Schleiermacher, *Hermeneutics: The Handwritten Manuscripts*, ed. Heinz Kinnerle, trans. James Duke and Jack Forstman, American Academy of Religion, Texts and Translation Series, no. 1. (Missoula, Mont.: Scholars Press, 1977).

if we adopt, as well, the other part of the standard view that it was Dilthey who first significantly expanded the scope of hermeneutics beyond that laid out by Schleiermacher, then it is obvious that what secondarily generated theorizing about interpretation was dissatisfaction with the obliviousness, exhibited by those who proposed constructing *Geisteswissenschaften* on the model of *Naturwissenschaften,* to the role of interpretation in human life.[2] Since human beings, unlike planets and viruses, interpret — pervasively and fundamentally so — any satisfactory *Geisteswissenschaft* will have to incorporate a theory of interpretation. Hermeneutics arose not out of pure intellectual wonder but out of a crisis in interpretative practice and out of dissatisfaction with scientistic obliviousness to its importance.

Why does it remain important? The importance of hermeneutics today lies in the fact that the crisis in the practice of biblical interpretation that spurred Schleiermacher's reflections has not only continued but deepened and spread, so that the practices used for interpreting a vast array of other texts are now similarly in crisis. Ironically, the causes of our present-day crises in the practices of text interpretation are in good measure those very theories of interpretation proposed for dealing with earlier crises. The importance of theorizing about interpretation today, to repeat, lies in the crises we are experiencing in the practices of interpreting texts, and not only biblical texts. These crises, in turn, have been caused by prior theorizing about interpretation. Hermeneutics spawns hermeneutics!

Many may be inclined, as a result of this situation, to pronounce a malediction on all their houses. But a malediction on their houses will not exorcise the spirits. There is no alternative but to engage the spirits.

It goes without saying that the Bible is important for our life as wayfarers and for our understanding of that life. Nor can we deny that in order to grasp the meaning and significance of the Bible for our lives, we have to *interpret* the Bible. If there are crises in biblical interpretation, those crises should concern Christians; if those crises are caused by the popularity of certain theories of interpretation, then those theories of interpretation should also concern Christians.

---

2. See Wilhelm Dilthey, *Poetry and Experience,* ed. Rudolf A. Makkreel and Frith-jof Rodi (Princeton: Princeton Univ. Press, 1985).

The Authorizing of Scripture

To put some flesh on these dry bones of abstraction, let us narrow our scope and sharpen our focus by concentrating on the practice of interpreting Scripture to find out what God said by way of authorizing that Scripture. There are, of course, many other ways of interpreting Scripture. Why focus on this one? In part because it provides an unusually good illustration of the intertwining of interpretive practice with interpretation theory. After being the dominant practice of biblical interpretation for more than 1,500 years, the practice went into severe decline around the time of the beginnings of modernity, and remains in decline. What caused the decline was, in good measure, the rise of hermeneutic theories incompatible with the practice. The revitalization of this practice is necessary for getting at what Scripture really is and for the vitality of the Christian community in the modern world.

To understand the importance of God's authorizing of Scripture, we begin by assuming that God not only reveals but speaks. Insofar as philosophers have discussed the topic of God speaking they have done so under the rubric of divine revelation; theologians, in good measure, have done the same. But we should not identify speaking with revealing. Take promising, for example. Suppose you wanted to analyze promising as a species of revealing; how would your analysis go? Presumably you would suggest that to promise to do something is to reveal that you intend to do it. But it is easy to see that that suggestion will not do. You can promise to do something without revealing that you intend to do it, because, for example, you do not intend to do it and so cannot reveal that you do. People do that sort of thing all the time. And conversely, you can reveal that you intend to do something without promising to do it; you may not want to bind yourself in the way that promising binds one.

Of course the person who wants to analyze promising as a species of revealing will not be devastated by these quick points; he will try to revise and complicate the analysis so as to circumvent the objections raised. Various stratagems might be devised to do this, but they will not work. To regard speaking as a species of revealing is to regard speaking as a mode of transmitting knowledge or of making something available to be known; and that is not, in general, what speaking is. It is always something more than that, and in such actions as promising and requesting, it is not at all that. Promising, when well formed, incorporates taking obligations onto oneself; requesting, when well formed, incorporates placing obligations on others. Neither of those consists of transmitting knowledge or of making something available to be known.

In saying that God speaks by way of authorizing Scripture, I assume that God *literally* speaks. That is to say, when I said that God speaks and does not just reveal, I want to be understood as having spoken literally, not metaphorically. I was not using a symbol. Of course, some people claim that God's nature or transcendence makes it impossible for us human beings, speaking literally, to affirm anything at all of God that is true of God; the only way to say something true of God while speaking literally is to deny things of God. This is a highly general objection that I will not deal with here. But I do wish to say something about the more specific objection that runs throughout the history of philosophy and theology, to the effect that it could not possibly be literally true of God that God speaks since God lacks the body necessary for speaking. God cannot speak, so it is said, because God has neither vocal cords with which to utter words nor limbs with which to write or sign words.

I think that now, finally, after all these centuries, contemporary speech action theory gives us the theoretical equipment to see why this objection does not hold water. Fundamental to speech action theory is the distinction between *locutionary* acts, *illocutionary* acts, and *perlocutionary* acts, to use the terminology introduced by J. L. Austin.[3] To understand God's speaking, we can neglect perlocutionary acts and focus just on locutionary and illocutionary acts. Suppose I ask you to open the door, and suppose, since we are both native speakers of English, that I do so by enunciating the English sentence, "Would you open the door?" Speech action theory proposes that in such a case we distinguish, within the totality of what I have done, two distinct acts. I have performed one action by performing another distinct action. Specifically, I have performed the action of asking you to open the door by performing the other action of enunciating the English sentence, "Would you open the door?" The former is an illocutionary act; the latter, a locutionary. I might have performed the illocutionary act of asking you to open the door in some other way than by performing the locutionary act of enunciating that English sentence. For example, I might have performed the locutionary

---

3. See J. L. Austin, *How to Do Things with Words,* ed. J. O. Urmson and Marina Sbisà, 2nd ed. (Cambridge: Harvard Univ. Press, 1975).

act of enunciating a synonymous sentence in some other language. Or I might have done so even without using language — by drawing a picture. Conversely, I might have enunciated that English sentence without thereby performing the illocutionary act of asking you to open the door; I might have enunciated it simply as an example of some point I was making. The fact that each of these actions can be performed without performing the other is what gives us reason to conclude that we are really dealing here with two distinct actions. But of course they are connected: I perform the one *by* performing the other.

This distinction between locutionary and illocutionary acts constitutes a liberating contribution to our thinking about divine speech. Confronted with the distinction, it is at once obvious that when we talk of God speaking, it is *illocutionary* acts that we want to be attributing to God. What we want to say about God is that God performs such illocutionary acts as issuing commands to us on our way, as well as promises and invitations to hope. Which actions are those actions that God performs so as thereby to perform these illocutionary acts is then another matter. Maybe God does not need a body to perform those generating acts. Suppose, for example, that God did in fact liberate Israel from her oppressors by leading her through wetlands onto dry ground. It does not seem that God needs a body to do that. But might God nonetheless not have been saying something thereby?

So far, then, we have two assumptions: That God speaks and does not just reveal, and that that is literally true. I wish to assume a third point, namely that God speaks by way of authorizing Scripture. That is not the only way God speaks. It is not even the most fundamental way; any Christian would want to say that God's speaking by way of Jesus Christ is more fundamental. But though it is neither the only way nor the most fundamental, nonetheless it is one extremely important way.

It was long and widely assumed in the history of the Christian church that God speaks by way of authorizing Scripture. Today, however, that view is intensely contested, within the church as well as without. Obviously the whole liberal tradition contests it. But I have concluded, to my surprise, that Karl Barth also contests it — this in spite of his hammering insistence on the centrality of the Word of God. Certainly Barth thought that God spoke and speaks by way of Jesus Christ. But close scrutiny of the structure of Barth's thought makes it clear that it was also his view that God speaks *only* in Jesus Christ. What was operating in Barth was the conviction, deep though seldom articulated, that only God's discourse can be the medium of divine discourse. It would compromise the sovereign freedom of God were anything else to be a medium of God's discourse; it would compromise God's freedom were anyone other than God to speak for God.

The Bible is truly indispensable for Christian existence, in part because you and I have no other access to God's speech in Jesus Christ than by way of the Bible, in part because, over and over, on the occasion of someone being confronted with some passage from the Bible, God convicts that person of the reality of his revelation in Jesus Christ.[4] But to say these two things is quite different from saying that God spoke by way of authorizing the Scriptures. And Barth did not say that; he did not want to say that, he resisted saying that. He did so because he thought it would be incompatible with God's freedom for God to speak by way of authorizing Scripture — but also because he thought that one could not acknowledge the legitimate results of historico-critical biblical scholarship if one said that. So the thesis that God spoke by way of authorizing the Bible is contested even in quarters where one would not, offhand, have expected it to be contested. Nonetheless it is a thesis that I take for granted so as to get on to other matters.

I must offer a few caveats to forestall misunderstanding. First, I do not by any means think that the only thing Christians should do with their Bibles is read them to find out what God said thereby. We should also take portions of the Bible on our own lips so as to express our own praise and penitence, thanksgiving and hope. We should, for example, appropriate the Psalms for ourselves by singing them. And we should internalize the metaphors and narratives and parables of the Bible so that they become for us lenses through which we ourselves see reality. The parable of the prodigal son, for example, is such a lens. It is not primarily a parable about a son who wastes an inheritance, however; it is primarily the parable of the *loathsome* son. Recall that the father is a pious Jewish father, and then listen: There was once a son who, when he had gotten himself into desperate straits by wasting all the money his father had given him, hired himself out to a Gentile pig farmer, living and eating among

---

4. See Karl Barth, *Church Dogmatics*, ed. G. W. Bromiley and T. F. Torrance, trans. G. T. Thomson et al., 4 vols. (Edinburgh: T. & T. Clark, 1936-1969), 1/2, pp. 583-85, 817; 1/3, pp. 200-204; 4/1, pp. 722-23; 4/2, pp. 303-4.

the pigs. That son, filthy and loathsome as anybody could be, was welcomed back with open arms by his father.

Second, when we are reading the Scriptures rather than using them in some other way, and when in our reading we are on the lookout for God's speech, we should be attentive not only to what God *said* by way of *authorizing* these Scriptures, but also to what God might here and now *be saying* by way of *presenting us* with a passage of Scripture. What God now says to us by way of presenting us with a biblical passage may be different from what God said by way of authorizing that passage. When St. Antony happened one day to be walking by, or standing in, a Coptic church, way back in the fourth century, he heard God then and there saying to him: You, Antony, distribute all your wealth to the poor and then follow me.

Third, it has long been a tenet of Judaism that God speaks anew in one's own day through the activity of midrashic interpretation of Scripture. We should recapture the counterpart conviction of the magisterial Reformers that God speaks in one's own day through the preacher's interpretation and proclamation of Scripture.

The First Blow against the Traditional Practice

With these caveats in mind, we can note that the first massive blow against the traditional practice of interpreting Scripture so as to find out what God had said thereby was delivered in the pre-Enlightenment era by people who were, in the main, eminently well intentioned toward the Bible. I have John Locke in mind, for example. Distinguish, if you will, between my using words so as *thereby* to promise, request, or assert something, and my using words to *transmit* a promise, request, or assertion already made by someone else or by myself on some other occasion. Locke and a good many of his cohorts consistently thought of the Bible along the latter lines. No doubt the fact that they almost always spoke of God revealing rather than of God speaking aided in obscuring the alternative from them.

Locke regarded the biblical writers as claiming to be reporters and recorders of prior episodes of divine revelation. The gospel writers reported what God had earlier revealed in Jesus Christ; St. Paul recorded what God had earlier revealed to him, and so forth. It was Locke's conviction that when the stakes are high, as they always are in matters of religion, it is our obligation never to believe just on their say-so what people claim, but to believe what they claim only after we have established, on the basis of evidence, that they are reliable on such matters. Locke himself was of the view that the results of this inquiry, in the case of the biblical writers, would be that they were in all likelihood inerrant in their reporting and recording of ancient revelation, as indeed on all other matters that they reported and recorded. There is no indication, in any of his published writings, that Locke himself ever undertook the project of collecting evidence for this conclusion; nonetheless, there can be no doubt that it was his view that were such a project to be undertaken, it would turn out highly probable that the biblical writers were inerrant.[5]

A fateful step had been taken, yet with what degree of wittingness it is difficult to tell. The Bible had been pried loose from the speech — or as Locke would prefer it, the *revelation* — of God; and that done, attention was focused entirely on the episodes of revelation that the Bible inerrantly reported and recorded. The book we have in hand, the Bible, was no longer regarded as itself an instrument of God's speech, but instead as a human record and report, inerrant because divinely inspired, of what God had said or revealed earlier and in some other way. It is deeply ironic that on this fateful move of prying the Bible loose from divine revelation and discourse, Karl Barth should have been in full agreement with John Locke!

I call the step fateful because there can be little doubt that it was that move, of prying the Bible loose from divine discourse and revelation, performed in the context of the Enlightenment insistence that on matters of maximal "concernment" we must not just believe people on their say-so, which proved to be the major impulse behind the rise of historico-critical study of the Bible. It is easy to see why it proved to be that. If you take the fundamental significance of the Bible to lie in its being a record and report of divine discourse and revelation, and if, furthermore, it is those episodes of divine discourse and revelation that are of prime

---

5. See John Locke, *An Essay Concerning Human Understanding*, ed. Peter H. Nidditch (Oxford: Clarendon Press, 1975); Locke, *The Reasonableness of Christianity*, ed. I. T. Ramsey (Stanford: Stanford Univ. Press, 1958); and W. Neil, "Criticism and the Theological Use of the Bible, 1700–1950," in *The Cambridge History of the Bible: The West from the Reformation to the Present Day*, ed. S. L. Greenslade, vol. 3 (Cambridge: Cambridge Univ. Press, 1963), pp. 240-41.

interest to you, and if you believe that on matters of such import one should never believe writers on their say-so, then obviously you are forced to consider the reliability of these reports. In the course of that consideration you will naturally bring everything you firmly believe into the picture. If you believe that miracles do not occur, then you will find yourself trying to get at the real events that lie behind the miracle stories in the Bible and offer hypotheses as to why the writers would have used miracle stories to describe nonmiraculous events. If you have convictions as to the criteria for a literary text being well composed and you assume that the biblical writers operated with the same criteria, and if you then find that the biblical text at certain junctures violates those criteria, you will speculate that the text was assembled by somewhat absent-minded redactors from previously existing documents that did satisfy those criteria. If you are of the theological conviction that God's economy moves from law to grace, and you find that the Old Testament text as we have it does not exhibit that pattern very well, you will propose a dating and reorganization that will exhibit it. If you find discrepancies in the biblical narratives, you will try to peer behind the discrepancies to see what really happened and will offer hypotheses as to why there are these discrepancies. And so forth.

I have called this whole cluster of inquiries the "historico-critical method" because that is what it is customarily called. But what impresses me, as someone looking in on the discipline from the outside, is how little there is of the historical, how much of the critical. So far as I can see, discoveries in the sands play a quite subordinate role; the discipline has been shaped almost entirely by theological convictions, by epistemological convictions, by convictions as to what does and does not happen in history, by assumptions of influence, and by literary and rhetorical convictions as to how reasonable human beings would and would not compose texts. Rather than being erected firmly on discoveries in the sands, the discipline strikes me, in good measure, as reflecting ourselves back to ourselves.

It is often said nowadays by critics of historical criticism that a good many of its practitioners are atheists. Probably some are, just as, given the evidence, probably some evangelical preachers are atheists! But I doubt that very many practitioners of historical criticism are atheists; I myself have never knowingly come across one such. Most practitioners of historical criticism would not even deny divine revelation. What is the case is that the life of its own which the discipline has acquired over the centuries leads fewer practitioners to attempt to identify ancient occurrences of divine revelation than was the case at the beginning.

An Evangelical-Critical Alliance

Many readers will have anticipated the point I want now to move on to make. The view of biblical interpretation that became characteristic if not definitive of Anglo-American evangelicalism shares with classic historical criticism those same Lockean assumptions to which I pointed; it is just located on the other end of the continuum of positions sharing those assumptions. Remember what those assumptions are: first, that the Bible is a record and report of ancient episodes of divine speech and revelation. Second, that our primary interest, once the Bible has been pried loose from divine revelation and discourse in this fashion, is not in the Bible per se but in that divine speech and revelation which it reports and records. And last, that when it comes to matters of maximal "concernment," nobody, not even a biblical writer, should be believed just on his or her own say-so. What we need is *evidence,* and *more* evidence, and *yet more* evidence.

The fundamental root of the difference between the evangelical position and that of the typical historical critic is their differing assessment of the evidence for the reliability of the biblical writers. The evangelical interprets the evidence available to us as pointing to inerrancy. And he concludes from this that the Bible came about by inspiration, on the ground that only divine inspiration could account for inerrancy on the sorts of matters that we find in the Bible. In turn, what especially leads the evangelical to differ from the historical critic, in his assessment of the evidence for reliability, is his difference of theological conviction as to how God works in history. The evangelical, unlike the typical historical critic, has no difficulty attributing to God the performance of miracles, nor any difficulty attributing to God the enabling of prophets to foretell the future. Where he does have serious difficulty, as it turns out, is in dealing with the apparent contradictions *within* the biblical text. One turns away in embarrassment from the unseemly attempts at harmonizing in which evangelical interpreters have engaged: two temple cleansings, six rooster-crowings, and so forth.

But rather than dwell on such points, let me instead observe that this evangelical application of the Lockean principles shares with the historico-critical application the trait of being destructive of the practice of reading the Bible so as to discern what God said by way of authorizing it. That claim will come as a surprise to many. The fact tends to be obscured from view by the prominence of inspiration within the evangelical account, and by the tendency to identify divine inspiration with divine speech.

Of course, the doctrine of inspiration has been a matter of notorious difficulty for evangelicals, mainly because the parameters set by the evangelical for the working of the Spirit insure that the results will seem very odd. The Spirit has to allow the personalities and cultural locations of the biblical writers to come to full expression while yet seeing to it that they are inerrant in what they say. We are told that the strategy of the Spirit for accomplishing this, in the case of Psalm 93, for example, was to inspire the writer to disbelieve the geocentric cosmology embraced by everybody around him while yet using the very same language that they all used to express that cosmology, using it then metaphorically rather than literally.

But whether or not a plausible doctrine of inspiration can be developed within the parameters given, what is to be noticed is that inspiration is in any case not the same as discourse. If in one way or another I inspire you to say what you say, it remains the case that *you* say it, not I. *You* perform the illocutionary act. One might wonder whether dictation does not constitute an exception to this general principle. Even if it did, that would not be of any help here, since the evident humanity of the Bible prevents the evangelical from claiming that inspiration took the form of dictation. But the point that must be made about dictation is that it is not inspiration. When a secretary takes dictation, she is not performing any illocutionary acts at all, and so is not *inspired* to perform any. In particular, she is not saying what her superior says when he eventually signs the letter. All she is doing is performing the *locutionary act* of writing down the words; it is he who performs the *illocutionary acts*. It is he who *says* things. St. Paul may well have used an amanuensis for his letter to the Romans; but it was Paul who was saying those things to the Roman Christians, not his amanuensis. Paul did not *inspire* his amanuensis to say things to the Roman Christians. So the point remains that for one person to inspire a second to say some things is not for the first person to say those things but for the second person to say them, and for the first person to have made a causal contribution to the second person's saying them. Divine inspiration is not to be identified with divine discourse.

The Second Blow against the Traditional Practice

A second massive blow has been inflicted on the traditional practice of biblical interpretation — this time in our own century, again by people who were completely well intentioned toward the Bible. Schleiermacher's view of interpretation — to put it very roughly and summarily — was that the goal of the interpreter is to enter into the life of the writer so as to understand what it was that the writer was expressing with his or her words. Discourse, at bottom, is self-expression in symbolic mode; and the goal of the interpreter is to traverse the trail of self-expression in reverse direction from that of the writer, so as to grasp the *intentions* of the writer.[6] The struggle to break loose from the grip of Schleiermacher's position has been the main dynamic behind twentieth-century hermeneutics. Whatever one's theory, one does not want interpretation to require delving into the intentions of the author. It is widely held that those intentions, for the most part, are inaccessible to interpreters, and it has been argued that even when they are accessible, they are irrelevant to interpretation.

So what is the alternative? The alternative, so almost all literary critics have supposed, is to aim at discovering *the sense* of the text. What is that? Well, let us grant, since we do in fact all take it for granted, that each of the well-formed sentences of a language has a *meaning*, a literal meaning. And then let us introduce the assumption that when a collection of well-formed sentences are put together seriatim into a literary unit, there emerges, for each sentence in the unit, a new thing, namely, a *contextual sense:* the sense of that sentence in that linguistic context. The *sense of the text* is then the totality of those contextual senses of its constituent sentences. Typically some of the sentences in the text will retain, as their contextual sense, the meaning that they have just by virtue of being well-formed sentences in the language. But the contextual sense of other sentences in the totality is likely to be metaphoric, or ironic, or hyperbolic — whatever is necessary for the totality of the sentences composing the text to make a coherent unit. *Textual-sense interpretation* consists then of interpreting a text with the aim in mind of discovering the sense of the text.

A good many people over the past twenty-five years have suggested

---

6. For a discussion of Schleiermacher on this point, see Joel C. Weinsheimer, *Gadamer's Hermeneutics: A Reading of "Truth and Method"* (New Haven: Yale Univ. Press, 1985), pp. 133-43.

that if biblical interpretation would reform itself to become textual-sense interpretation, the crises and conflicts in which it finds itself would in good measure be dissipated. The two most influential of those who have made this suggestion have probably been Hans Frei and Paul Ricoeur.

Frei was struck by the fact that if one looked carefully at what biblical critics said about the function of the biblical narratives, and if one then asked oneself what one would expect a text playing that function to be like, it turned out over and over that the texts of the biblical narratives are not like that at all. Over and over there was a singularly inept mismatch between these actual texts and the function that they were said to be playing. It was said, for example, that they were mythical in their function. But we have texts of myths from the Greeks, the Romans, and the Norse, and the biblical narratives are strikingly unlike those. What struck Frei, in short, was how little attention biblical critics paid to the actual narratives of Scripture.

Why is that, he asked? His answer points to some of the same features of the Lockean theory and practice that I pointed to: the prying loose of the Bible from divine discourse and revelation, the construal of the Bible as record and report of ancient divine revelation, and the assumption that what is of interest, as between the report of the revelation and the revelation itself, is of course the revelation. Frei's way of putting all of this was to say that *meaning* was mistakenly assumed to be *reference;* and he set himself the project, in his *Eclipse of Biblical Narrative,* of tracing what happened when critics became more and more skeptical as to the accuracy of the Bible's reports of revelation, but wanted, nonetheless, to regard the Bible as deeply meaningful. Eventually critics proposed, as the "true referent" of biblical narrative, something very different indeed from events in the historical past; namely, mythically formulated insight into our human condition.[7] This brings us to where Frei began, that is, to the severe lack of fit between that function and these texts.

So what are we to do? Practice textual-sense interpretation, said Frei. The root of what had gone wrong was that interpreters had taken the point of these narratives — in Frei's terminology, the *meaning* — to lie outside of the narratives, back in ancient history. Ax the tree at its root. Make discerning the *sense* of these narratives the goal of one's interpretation. They mean what they say, said Frei. By which he did not mean that they say what

---

7. See Hans W. Frei, *The Eclipse of Biblical Narrative: A Study in Eighteenth and Nineteenth Century Hermeneutics* (New Haven: Yale Univ. Press, 1974), pp. 9-16.

they intend to say. Recall the point I made just above, that Frei called *the point* of a narrative its *meaning*. His thesis is that the point of these narratives is what they say: their point is their sense, not their reference.[8] And the basic pattern of their sense, Frei went on to argue, is Jesus' enactment of his messiahship or Jesus' enactment of the breaking in of the kingdom. Putting it into words is not easy; some of the options seem equally good. What we must keep in mind, though, is that the theme is a narrative theme. Divine-human reconciliation is not even a candidate for being the theme, since it carries no echo whatsoever of narrativity; by contrast, Jesus' enactment of divine-human reconciliation bears consideration.

What we must also keep in mind is that the narrative theme, whatever we eventually settle on as the best statement thereof, will have Jesus of Nazareth at its center. That is to say, it will have *the character Jesus* as its center. Remember that in our interpretative endeavors we are to concentrate exclusively on textual sense.

Yet Frei did not himself believe that it is only the story that is important, nor only the character Jesus. He believed that what was truly important was the actual Jesus Christ — God incarnate. And it was an important part of his full view that the Gospel narratives constitute both our best access to that Chalcedonian reality, and an entirely adequate access.

But given those convictions, what are we to make of Frei's claim that the Gospel narratives mean what they say, that their point is just their sense? Unless Frei has inadvertently abandoned that claim, which does not seem likely, we are forced to the conclusion that what Frei thought ultimately important about these narratives was something other than their point. For though it is their sense that is their point, it is not their sense that is ultimately important for Frei. What is important is the reality outside of their sense which that sense presents to us: the actual historical person Jesus Christ.

Is this really any different from taking their meaning, their point, to be their reference? Has not Frei in fact been forced into the very position that he regarded as the root of all interpretative evils, that of taking meaning to be reference? My guess is that Frei would attempt to wriggle out by saying that he does not regard reference to the actual Jesus Christ as the point of the narrative; the point of the narrative remains its own internal sense. Rather, those of us who are Christians, once our interpretation of the sense

8. Frei, *Eclipse of Biblical Narrative*, pp. 279-81.

is completed, find ourselves strangely compelled to *treat* that sense as presenting to us a man from Nazareth. That is not the meaning of the narrative as such; the narrative's meaning remains its internal sense. It is a meaning we give to the narrative, a role it comes to play in our lives. Along these lines Frei would be likely to reply. I doubt that anybody other than Frei finds the reply satisfactory. I even rather doubt that he himself did.

It may seem surprising to associate closely the projects of Frei and Ricoeur. After all, Frei spent a good deal of the time and energy of his latter years distancing himself from Ricoeur. Still, there can be no doubt at all that Frei and Ricoeur were united in being determined advocates of biblical interpretation as textual-sense interpretation. In fact, Ricoeur mounted an elaborate argument for the thesis that all interpretation of texts, biblical or not, that occurs at a distance from the time, place, and person of their composition, has to be textual-sense interpretation. Authorial-intent interpretation was the only alternative that he recognized; and though he thought that one might be successful in discerning the intention of a discourser when one is in her presence at the time and place of discourse, he argued implacably that there is no hope whatsoever of success at discerning authorial intention when one is interpreting at a distance. Interpretation at a distance can only be textual-sense interpretation.

What must at once be added is that Ricoeur regarded the sense of a text — at least the sense of a literary or religious text — as always pointing beyond itself. It always projects a way of being in the world, a mode of existence, a pattern of life. It always has a reference, of a sort. One might ask whether this reference is part of the sense. Perhaps not a *part;* but certainly it is a supervenient feature thereof. The sense of a text does not contingently *acquire* such a reference; it *has* it, intrinsically. Textual-sense interpretation, accordingly, must include the attempt to discern this reference-of-the-sense of the text. That is true especially for interpretation of religious texts. The reference-of-the-sense of the Gospel narratives is that way of being in the world which may be called *the kingdom of God;* our interpretation of the Gospels, whatever else it does, must aim at illuminating that reference.[9]

9. See Paul Ricoeur, *Interpretation Theory: Discourse and the Surplus of Meaning* (Fort Worth: Texas Christian Univ. Press, 1976), pp. 1-23, and *Hermeneutics and the Human Sciences,* ed. and trans. John B. Thompson (Cambridge: Cambridge Univ. Press, 1981), pp. 145-93.

That Frei polemicized against Ricoeur should now be no surprise. The kingdom of God as the point of the Gospels: with such a view, all the narrativity is gone. Frei regarded Ricoeur's suggestion as yet one more example of the infection whose sting he had spent his whole career trying to pull. That obscured from him the fact that, in essentials, he and Ricoeur were blood brothers.

The Myth of the Sense of a Text

We can leave it to the followers of Frei and Ricoeur to argue the disagreements between their masters. What is important to note is that, no matter which variant one prefers, to suppose that textual-sense interpretation gives us the right way of interpreting the Bible is automatically to place the traditional practice of biblical interpretation under attack. To show why that is the case, let me begin by arguing that there is no such thing as *the sense* of a text.

We saw earlier that the core idea behind the notion of *the sense of a text* is that the very activity of fitting sentences together into a literary unit supposedly allows some of those sentences to keep their literal meaning, forces others to acquire an ironic meaning, forces yet others to acquire a metaphoric meaning, and so forth. In short, this activity supposedly forces a definite meaning upon the totality, with due allowance for a few ambiguities. But it is easy to see that it does not do so. For one thing, why assume that texts are coherent, that they hang together; why can there not be breaks, incoherences, contradictions? This point is made by the deconstructionists — *ad nauseam,* I admit, but true nonetheless. Second, even if one insists on arriving at an interpretation that renders the text coherent, that insistence always leaves one with a multiplicity of options as to which sentences to take as literal and which as metaphoric. The choice is not forced. John Locke wrote the sentence, "Reason is the candle of the Lord."[10] One naturally interprets this as metaphoric speech because we all naturally read for what the author said. But if we are just taking the sentences of the text and trying to come up with a coherent interpretation of the whole, why not interpret that sentence as literal and then, in consequence, interpret a whole range of others as metaphoric? The result would be mad, you say!

10. See Locke, *Reasonableness of Christianity,* para. 231.

So it would. But so what? I submit that if all we allow ourselves to go on is sentential meaning, then there is no stopping place short of the point where full permission is granted to that deconstructionist play of interpretations on which the only constraint is the *de facto* constraint of lack of imagination.

But why not bite the bullet and make biblical interpretation a species of the play-of-interpretations style of interpretation? Here and there nowadays one finds the suggestion popping up. Well, suppose it appears to you that someone is promising you something; suppose further that you very much care whether or not they are promising, and if they are, *what* they are. The relevant mode of interpretation is obviously that which consists of trying to discern what he or she promised. Or to generalize, it is that which consists of trying to discern what illocutionary action he or she performed. Call such interpretation *authorial discourse interpretation*. The play-of-interpretations style of interpretation will not get you there. Its whole point is to exercise one's imagination. There is nothing wrong with exercising one's imagination. But it does not get one in touch with what someone said. For that, what is needed, to say it again, is *authorial discourse interpretation*. It is worth adding that Derrida, the master deconstructionist, insists that when we interpret *his* texts, we must interpret for *what he said*. He insists that we interpret for authorial discourse.

The analogue is pretty obvious. Suppose you believe that the Scriptures are a medium of divine discourse. It is hard for me to imagine anyone who really believes this but has no interest in finding out what it is that God said by way of Scripture. Now if there were a sense of a text and if it were identical with what a person said by way of authoring the text, then interpreting for the sense of the text would, when successful, automatically yield a grasp of the authorial discourse. What ultimately underlies Ricoeur's whole strategy is his assumption that there is that identity of textual sense with authorial discourse. But we have just seen that there is no such thing as *the* sense of a text; textual sense is a many-splintered thing. So if you do believe that the Scriptures are a medium of divine discourse, then what is wanted is authorial discourse interpretation. Nothing else will do. Not textual-sense interpretation, and not play-of-interpretations interpretation.

But does not the adoption of authorial discourse interpretation amount to jumping out of the frying pan into the fire? Are we not beset with all of the difficulties attendant on trying to delve into the inner recesses of an author's consciousness so as to discern authorial intentions? Not at all. Reading to discern authorial intentions and reading to discern textual sense do not exhaust the alternatives. We have to liberate ourselves from the grip of the notion that there is nothing between Romanticism and Structuralism. In addition to an author's intentions, and in addition to an author's text, there is what the author did in fact say by authoring his text. Not what he *intended* to say; what he *did* say. We do in fact say things. We do not just form intentions to say things, and compose texts; we say things, often by means of texts. So we can set as the goal of our interpretation discerning what an author said. And that is what I have been calling *authorial discourse* interpretation. Of course it is true that intentions are involved in the performance of illocutionary actions; an illocutionary action is inherently an intentional action — not an action that one intends to perform, but an intentional action. So the Romantics were on to something. But there is no reason at all to suppose that the relevant intentions are buried deep inside our psyches, forever beyond the prying eyes of neighbors.

Double Discourse

Authorial discourse interpretation cannot even get going on Scripture, however, without some understanding of how the human and divine dimensions in Scripture are related. So let me move on to make a suggestion on this score.

Notice that sometimes one person says something by way of another person saying something. Double discourse, call it. The Bible confronts us with double discourse. Such discourse comes in two significantly different forms. Sometimes one person speaks on behalf of another, or in the name of another: an ambassador on behalf of his head of state, an attorney in the name of his client. Ancient Israel understood the prophets as speaking on behalf of God and in the name of God. Their speech was *deputized* speech. By way of hearing the prophet say something, an auditor heard God saying something. No doubt the prophets also transmitted messages from God; but that, as we saw earlier, is different. One can transmit a message from someone only if that person has already spoken that message. Not only did the prophets tell the people what God had already said to them; God spoke to the people by way of the speaking of the prophets. Prophetic speech was one of the media of divine speech.

We recognize the other kind of double discourse in such familiar

remarks as "I second the motion," "She speaks for me, too," "As de Tocqueville so perceptively remarked," and "I couldn't agree more." In such
cases, one person *appropriates* the discourse of another for his own. The
other person did not speak in my name or on my behalf; I simply take what
she has already said and appropriate it. The best way to understand how it
is that the Bible can be an instrument of divine discourse, in its prophetic
as well as its nonprophetic parts, is to understand it in its totality as a blend
of *deputized* and *appropriated* discourse.

A feature of double discourse that, for our purposes, is extremely
important to notice is that the deputizer or appropriator may disagree with,
or disapprove of, various things in the deputized or appropriated discourse
while yet genuinely deputizing or appropriating it. An attorney may genuinely
be representing his client even though the client does not agree with everything his attorney is saying nor approve of everything in how he is saying it.
And I can approvingly quote a passage from de Tocqueville without agreeing
with the passage in all of its details. The application of these points to human
speech on behalf of God and to human speech appropriated by God is
obvious: God can speak by way of the infirm and fallible speech of us human
beings. The doctrine of biblical inerrancy amounts to claiming that everything said by any biblical author was said by God. Evangelicals entered a dead
end when they committed themselves to that doctrine. What matters is not
Daniel's inerrancy but God's infallibility.

The interpretative corollary of double discourse is a double hermeneutic. Let me concentrate on appropriated (rather than deputized) discourse: to discover what the appropriator was saying, one must first discern
the stance and content of the appropriated discourse, and then move on
from there to discerning the stance and content of the appropriating discourse. From among the many things that might be said about this move
in the case of biblical interpretation, let me single out just two.

The Bible is not to be thought of as God's *opera omnia* — some
sixty-six of God's works collected together. It is to be thought of as one
volume of some sixty-six parts, or chapters, or books, call them what you
will. What this implies, for the practice of interpretation, is that the relevant
context of interpretation changes radically as one moves from the appropriated human discourse to the appropriating divine discourse. Suppose
that I select a short story, a poem, a theological discourse, and a philosophical treatise, bundle them all together, and send them off to a friend with
the indication that these four taken together give what I want to say to her.

If my friend is to discern what I said, she will have to read all four together, interpreting each in the light of the other. The Song of Solomon has its own integrity; it is important, in the first stage of the double hermeneutic, to honor that integrity. But then one moves on to interpret the Song in the context of the Christian canon. Biblical critics sometimes talk as if one has to choose between interpreting passages in the context of a biblical book, or some unit even smaller than that, and interpreting them in the context of the canon. The truth is that both contexts of interpretation are called for, to be used in succession.

Second, in the move from the human appropriated discourse to the divine appropriating discourse, we must bring into play our knowledge of who God is. We must, for example, allow ourselves to be guided by those two principles of biblical interpretation laid down by Augustine in his *de doctrina Christiana:* Never to interpret God as speaking falsely, and never to interpret God as speaking unlovingly.[11] So as to honor these principles, we will sometimes find ourselves interpreting a sentence as literal, when we are considering what the human writer said thereby, and interpreting that same sentence as metaphorical, when considering what God said thereby. One of the best ways to see how this would work is to take a good translation of the Psalms in one hand, Isaac Watts' versification of the Psalms for singing in the church in the other hand, and then compare the two.

There is a streak of radical Protestantism that holds that we are not to bring any of our beliefs about God *to* our interpretation of Scripture but are instead to get all of them *from* our interpretation of Scripture. It cannot work; interpretation of someone's discourse can only occur in the context of already knowing something about that person. Biblical interpretation could not even get going if we did not, as a sheer minimum, presuppose that God speaks consistently. Yet the worry behind the radical Protestant principle points to an important truth. We constantly run the risk of making of Scripture a wax nose. God has not given us any foolproof method for circumventing this danger. But God has given us a way of minimizing it: interpretation of Scripture must go hand in hand with cultivation of the devotional practices for knowing God.

All of this is only a sketch. In *Divine Discourse,* I have filled in a great many of the details in both this double hermeneutic and in my argumen-

---

11. See Augustine, *On Christian Doctrine,* trans. D. W. Robertson, Jr. (Indianapolis: Bobbs-Merrill, 1958), 3.10.14; 3.16.24.

tation against the alternative hermeneutics.[12] I hope, however, that even without the details, I have not only succeeded in displaying the importance of hermeneutics in our Christian existence, but in pointing toward a hermeneutic that is not only viable in general but appropriate to the conviction that God spoke in ancient times by way of appropriating the discourse of Amos and Micah, Matthew and Paul, and all of the other biblical writers taken together.

12. Nicholas Wolterstorff, *Divine Discourse: Philosophical Reflections on the Claim that God Speaks* (Cambridge: Cambridge Univ. Press, 1995).

"To Find Out What God Is Saying": Reflections on the Authorizing of Scripture

I. HOWARD MARSHALL

Many of the Christian church's problems with regard to Scripture are matters of hermeneutics rather than of authority and inspiration. For example, this would be the case with our understanding of creation in relation to the Genesis account and to the findings of science. It is also the case where God's principles for godly living are expressed in particular terms appropriate to Old Testament times or to first-century Corinth.

Rather than being primarily concerned with the importance of hermeneutics as an express theme, Nicholas Wolterstorff seeks to illustrate the importance of hermeneutics by discussing how to interpret Scripture and by showing what happens when we do it rightly and wrongly. Some writers on hermeneutics have thought that they have accomplished their duty simply by attempting to describe and analyze what people actually do in interpretation. Basic though that is, it cannot be the whole task; we also need to ask what we ought to do and ought not to do, and Wolterstorff makes some important recommendations on this.

Particularly helpful is the way that he reinstates the task of interpreting Scripture to find out what *God* is saying. This is the proper, ultimate task of Christian interpretation. Whether this can be done only within the Christian framework is another question, but he is surely right to insist on the need to know God better in order to understand what he says better.

Wolterstorff also offers us a method of understanding the nature of Scripture that helps us to deal with the difficult fact that the Bible contains a variety of materials that are hardly divine revelation, in the sense of God speaking directly to us or revealing himself to us. These include not only the places where human beings praise God, but also the places where people — such as Job's friends — ask questions about God or make statements about him that are not right. It is a merit of the theory that it allows God to authorize this material as something that he wants to be recorded for our benefit, so that we may use it as a pattern for our praise or as a warning against wrong sentiments.

God and Scripture

While Wolterstorff makes a vital attempt to chart a course for the interpretation of Scripture, his argument raises crucial questions. He appears to have two main things to say in this essay, and we need to ask whether they are organically related, so that neither stands unless the other stands also.

The first of Wolterstorff's points is the relation of God to the human writers of Scripture. He suggests that there are two kinds of material. There is the case of "deputized speech," when God tells somebody what to say and that person later says, "The Word of the Lord came to me, saying. . . ." And there is the case of "appropriated speech," where a person says something, and God in effect says "Amen, brother [rarely "sister" in the Bible], to that. I couldn't put it better myself!" Where the evangelical tradition speaks of God being the author of Scripture, as we say on our side of the Atlantic, or "authoring Scripture," as Americans tend to say, Wolterstorff refers to God "authorizing Scripture." The model that immediately comes to mind is that of the Pope or his representative being willing to print at the beginning of a book *"Nihil obstat"* or *"Imprimatur."*

This way of understanding Scripture as a whole as "appropriated discourse" raises a number of problems for reflection. First, there is the curiosity that Scripture contains both of the kinds of material that we have mentioned side by side. A prophetic book is a mixture of the two sorts of speech. In some passages the prophet records what he heard as a word from the Lord, and in other passages the prophet himself writes as the framework for the Lord's words, and may include his own meditations and his own words addressed to the Lord; the book of Jeremiah presents this combination very clearly. But this means that in the case of the sayings that the prophet heard directly from the Lord there would appear to be a sense in which God appropriates what he has already deputed, as if he were granting approval to his own words. I find a tension here. It may be partly resolved by claiming that God approves and appropriates the prophet's rendering of his sayings, which may well not be a verbatim account of what he said, but this does not wholly relieve the tension.

In addition, there is the problem of what is going on during the time when a biblical writer is not acting as the deputy but is composing on his own. What makes that person function in such a way as to produce material that God will be able to authorize? Why is it that God presumably authorized some of what Paul wrote in his letters, namely the extant ones, but did not authorize that earlier letter to Corinth that preceded 1 Corinthians or that lost Letter to the Laodiceans? Wolterstorff's hypothesis deals with the divine activity that takes place after the words that he is going to appropriate have been composed, but at least in this address, it does not shed any light on the actual composition. There is thus a gap in the explanation, in that we have been offered no theory as to how people are able to write material that God is going to authorize one day. We have, as it were, transferred the divine action, which is apparently one of passive approval, to after the speaking, instead of, as traditionally, being an action that somehow influences the speaker and does so before or during the speech. But it is obvious that not all human speech, not even that of "holy men of old," is of a kind that God can appropriate. What, if anything, is there different about the speech that he does appropriate?

That, in turn, raises the question of when and how the divine authorizing takes place. The language is no doubt metaphorical, but what is the reality that is being described metaphorically? Are we thinking of the process of canonization and identifying that with the divine authorization? But that can hardly be the case, because the traditional view of canonization, which I believe to be the correct view, is that the church recognized the inherent authority of the books that it canonized; it did not confer authority on them. The books were authoritative as expressions of God's word long before they were canonized. Canonization, too, was a lengthy process rather than a punctiliar decision. So canonization as a process by which God authorizes Scripture, guiding the church to recognize the authority of certain writings, will not work. Canonization is not the same thing as inspiration. Canonization is the church's recognition, doubtless under the guidance of the Spirit, of those books which God has already authorized. But when did he authorize them? Does God say that he is doing so anywhere in Scripture?

Finally, evangelicals will want to ponder carefully before they accept the suggestion that God can appropriate what is in some ways faulty and take it over without approving of it completely. This, of course, is not to say that the model of divine authorization as opposed to divine authoring is introducing a new problem. Evangelicals who believe in the divine authoring of Scripture already have a problem, however they may try to solve it. If God approves of the writings of, say, Obadiah, he is approving of a limited, one-sided, and partial revelation, and therefore the approval can only be in the context of a limited purpose for the book at a given period in time when it was necessary only to make certain, limited truths known, and also in the context of his total acceptance of Scripture, which enables us to see that there are other necessary things to be said alongside what is said through Obadiah.

In dealing with this problem, Wolterstorff produces an understanding of Scripture basically similar to that of Emil Brunner, who used the analogy of our listening to a gramophone record that has various scratches on it that prevent us from hearing the sound with complete accuracy. And of course we are still left with the problem of how we know to what extent God was prepared to say his "Amen" to all that a given biblical author said.

It is doubtful, therefore, whether Wolterstorff's hypothesis succeeds any better in reconciling the existence of apparent historical, doctrinal, and moral difficulties in the Bible by saying that God's appropriation does not imply total approval any more than do the older theories of inspiration that have to reckon with progress in revelation. It may be that Wolterstorff's understanding of the nature of Scripture actually raises fresh problems for us and leaves some of the traditional ones in much the same situation as before.

The Meaning of the Text

The other side of Wolterstorff's thesis is its understanding of language with the distinction between illocutionary and locutionary acts. It is important to remember, however, that a third category comes into the discussion of speech acts, namely perlocutionary acts. A perlocutionary act is one in which you cause something to happen through speaking as an act of power, and it has in mind the effect produced on the other person, such as making him or her feel embarrassed. An illocutionary act is an act done in speaking, one in which you do something by speaking, such as asking a person to do something or warning him or her, or making a promise, and a locutionary act is simply the action of uttering the words that make up a meaningful act of speaking.[1]

Now in the philosophy of J. L. Austin, from which these concepts come, illocutionary acts are performed by utterance. The two are separable to the extent that the letter-writer may use a secretary to write down the words. The novelty of Wolterstorff's proposal is that in the case of God it separates the illocutionary from the locutionary, so that instead of God himself speaking he can produce the illocutionary effect by using the locutionary acts of other people whose speech he authorizes. Thus the concept of the locutionary act is extended, or perhaps understood metaphorically, in order to accommodate the divine action.

It is hard to quarrel with this possibility, but there are problems with the discussion of what Wolterstorff calls the sense of the text. He says that a discourse consists of well-formed sentences; we can get the meaning of each in its context; and the sense of the discourse is the sense of the collection of sentences as a whole.

Wolterstorff then suggests that Hans Frei denies that the referents of the biblical texts are either things that actually happened (because on Frei's view the Bible is inaccurate) or "mythologically formulated insights into our human condition." According to Frei, the point of the texts is what they say. And what they say is a narrative theme, namely, Jesus' enactment of divine-human reconciliation. If I have grasped correctly what Frei is doing, according to Wolterstorff, it is to insist that the point of the text, that is, its meaning, is simply what the texts say, rather than that to which they refer, and yet in the end of the day what matters for Frei is in fact something outside of the texts, namely Jesus.[2]

By contrast Paul Ricoeur says that we are to get back to what the author intended. Yet the text does have a point of reference outside of itself, which for Ricoeur is the kingdom of God. It points to a way of life, rather than to something that is expressed by narrative.[3]

---

1. See J. L. Austin, *How to Do Things with Words*, ed. J. O. Urmson and Marina Sbisà, 2nd ed. (Cambridge: Harvard Univ. Press, 1975).

2. See Hans Frei, *The Eclipse of Biblical Narrative: A Study in Eighteenth and Nineteenth Century Hermeneutics* (New Haven: Yale Univ. Press, 1974), pp. 9-16, 279-81.

3. See Paul Ricoeur, *Hermeneutics and the Human Sciences*, ed. and trans. John B. Thompson (Cambridge: Cambridge Univ. Press, 1981), pp. 145-93.

Wolterstorff then proceeds to say, "a plague on both your houses," and goes on to deny that a text has a sense. He appears to do this because of the ambiguity that is discerned in many texts. That is, different interpreters interpret them in different ways. He resolves the problem by recourse to "authorial discourse interpretation," which he explains as "trying to discern what illocutionary act the author performed." Or what did the author do in fact by authoring the text?

This solution is puzzling, because it takes things that belong to different categories and treats them as if they were separate possibilities within a single category. But why do we have to go for only one of the three possibilities, the reference, *or* the sense, *or* what the author is doing? The problem is that these things which Wolterstorff treats as alternatives are surely different aspects of the same process or the same text. It is a perfectly fair question to ask, "What was the author doing by this illocutionary act?" One answer may be, "He was giving information about the deeds of Jesus," or another may be, "He was telling us how we ought to live." Now these are different illocutionary acts, teaching and persuasion perhaps. But common to both of these illocutionary acts is the transmission of factual content, such as certain specific stories about Jesus rather than others, or descriptions of certain specific types of moral action that we ought to practice. So there is a "content" aspect to the discourse as well as an illocutionary force. Also, a question of reference may arise in various ways. Was there a "Jesus" who is the historical referent of the stories, and are the stories themselves correctly recorded? What specific actions are being recommended, as compared with other possible candidates, and is the doing of them right and therefore an obligation that should be laid upon us?

A number of complementary questions, all of them legitimate, need to be asked here. The root of the confusion may be that there is a danger, into which perhaps Frei and Ricoeur fall, of trying to get a single formula that will fit the whole of the Bible. It is not so. Some texts may be about Jesus as the referent (a description), others may be about a particular set of events (a narrative), and yet others may be about a set of ethical rules or recommendations (may we call them commands and assert that they "exist" in the sense that they may be the commands of God?).

In short, the use of modern theory of language to help us to understand the nature of God's speech in Scripture is currently providing fresh light. Others, alongside Wolterstorff, have recognized its potential. I cite one example. In 1994 we celebrated an interesting double anniversary, the five-hundredth anniversary of the birth of William Tyndale, who probably did more than any other person to make the Scriptures accessible and intelligible in the English language, and the jubilee of the Tyndale Fellowship for Biblical Research. The jubilee conference led to the publication of a set of papers, which include an important essay on "God's Mighty Speech-Acts: The Doctrine of Scripture Today" by Kevin Vanhoozer,[4] which may be seen as complementary to Wolterstorff's paper in that it explores the category of divine speech-acts in relation to the writing of Scripture as contrasted with its divine authorization. It is clear, therefore, that the debate among the philosophers and theologians will continue, and biblical scholars like myself will look forward with eagerness to what can be learned from it. For in the end of the day, it is of crucial importance for us to know in what sense the Bible is the Word of God to us and how the words of human beings can be the vehicles of the divine acts of speech that proclaim his gracious gift of salvation and summon us to live under his lordship.

4. P. E. Satterthwaite and D. F. Wright, eds., *A Pathway into the Holy Scripture* (Grand Rapids: Eerdmans, 1994), pp. 143-81.

Post-Kantian Reflections on the
Importance of Hermeneutics

MEROLD WESTPHAL

W e used to have a pastor who prefaced each Scripture lesson with the admonition, "Listen *for* the word of God." That way of putting it reminded me more effectively that I was about to be addressed than did the formula with which I was both more familiar and more comfortable: "Listen *to* the word of God." But it also suggested to me that the pastor was not comfortable with saying, simply, "The Bible is the word of God." Nicholas Wolterstorff, I gather, does not share that discomfort. The whole point of his book *Divine Discourse,* from which the essay in this volume is derived, is to try to make sense of the claim that the Bible is the word of God and to make sense of the interpretive practices that go with such a claim.

It seems to me that his overall project has two goals, corresponding to two audiences. He wants to persuade those to his theological left that unless they have a subtheistic conception of God there are no intellectual and conceptual barriers to the belief that God speaks to us in and through the Bible. The obstacles to such belief are only *prima facie* and can be overcome. And he wants to persuade those to his theological right that in order to maintain the claim that the Bible is the word of God, in and through which God speaks to us today, it is not necessary to wed this view to stronger, less tenable views such as inerrancy. By seeking a middle way between those with too weak a view and those with too strong a view of divine discourse, he pretty well guarantees that he will get shot at from both sides.

My task is to keep his life from getting boring by seeing to it that a few shots are fired from a third direction. I am sympathetic with his overall project. I share his belief that the interpretive practice he seeks to revitalize is "necessary for getting at what Scripture really is and for the vitality of the Christian community in the modern world." I agree that God "not only reveals but speaks," that "God *literally* speaks," that "God speaks by authorizing Scripture," and that speech act theory in general and double discourse theory in particular provide useful conceptual tools for thinking about these matters.

My agreements with Wolterstorff go beyond those I have just cited, but there may be philosophical differences between us that are important to the matters at hand. For example, I find nothing in Ricoeur or Derrida incompatible with a plausible hermeneutics of authorial discourse; but this presupposes readings of these two thinkers rather different from Wolterstorff's. I want to focus, however, on a difference I take to be considerably more basic. The framework within which he develops his argument is pre-Kantian, even though he thinks of himself as post-Kantian. As a chronological claim I will not dispute it; but as a philosophical claim I am not so sure. His pre-Kantianism is so far from being naïve that I am tempted to call it stubborn.

Wolterstorff begins by acknowledging that interpretation is so pervasive in human life that to speak of it as deliberate, agonized, and contested is to focus on only one end of the spectrum. Most of the time we do not set out to interpret, much less seek to overcome some crisis of interpretation. We just interpret, habitually, unreflectively, and more or less unproblematically. In the case of the Bible, however, we do set out to interpret, quite deliberately; and the only reason I can think of for denying that there is *a* crisis in biblical interpretation today is that there are so many of them. So it is natural that Wolterstorff focuses on what he calls agonized (in both senses, *agon* and *agony*) interpretation. At one time this branch of hermeneutics concerned itself primarily with legal and biblical interpretation; but recent cultural developments have rendered the interpretation of literary texts at least as agonizing, again, in both senses.

Without seeking in any way to diminish the importance of all this agony for our culture in general or of Wolterstorff's question for the Christian church, I want to suggest that the other end of the hermeneutical spectrum, the one that focuses on prereflective interpretation, raises issues of enormous importance for a Christian worldview in general and for Wolterstorff's project in particular. The philosophical hermeneutics of

Heidegger and Gadamer can be called a theory of interpretation, but it conspicuously does not focus on the question, "How should we set out to interpret . . . ?" It rather asks what interpretation is and what role it plays in human experience, prior to those occasions when we set out to interpret.

The Nature of Interpretation

As for the question of the nature of interpretation, the importance of hermeneutics for Christian thinking is to be understood more broadly than when Wolterstorff says, "The importance of theorizing about interpretation today lies in the crises we are experiencing in the practices of interpreting texts."

The account of what interpretation is that is given by Heidegger and Gadamer conforms closely with Wolterstorff's account. What is at issue is construal, whether one speaks, with Gadamer, of seeing something as something or, with Wolterstorff, of making something of something. The central point is that the phenomenon that is construed when we make something of it or see it as something underdetermines its interpretation and does not dictate it. (It is helpful here to think of the famous duck-rabbit figure that Wittgenstein borrows from Jastrow, as well as two concepts closely related to underdetermination: uncertainty as used by Heisenberg and undecidability as used by Gödel and Derrida).[1] This underdetermination is what Wolterstorff refers to when he describes interpretation as the activity "whereby we traverse that open space of alternative possibilities." This open space is created because "the phenomenon in question does not automatically produce" the action or knowledge that its interpretation gives rise to, and because "our experience and perception of the items of reality leave open what we are to make of those items."

This means that interpretation is not at all like deductive inference, that it is more like formulating an empirical hypothesis than like testing it by the canons of inductive logic, and is importantly similar to generating a metaphor.

The underdetermination of interpretation by the phenomenon being

---

1. The duck-rabbit appears on p. 194 of Ludwig Wittgenstein, *Philosophical Investigations*, trans. G. E. M. Anscombe, 2nd ed. (Oxford: Blackwell, 1963). Derrida explicitly links his concept of undecidability to Gödel. See Jacques Derrida, *Writing and Difference*, trans. Alan Bass (Chicago: Univ. of Chicago Press, 1978), p. 162, and *Dissemination*, trans. Barbara Johnson (Chicago: Univ. of Chicago Press, 1981), p. 219.

interpreted is well illustrated by the first example Wolterstorff cites, the interpretation of a musical score. There seems to be wide and well-grounded agreement about two points here. First, there is no such thing as *the* interpretation of a given piece, since a variety of interpretations are compatible with what the score clearly requires and are judged to be musically competent and sensitive by those best able to make discriminating judgments. A plurality of quite different interpretations will merit such praise as nuanced, brilliant, illuminating, path-breaking, epochal, and so forth, though none will be referred to as *the right* interpretation. Second, it does not at all follow that anything goes or that one interpretation is as good as another. If I play G# where the score calls for an F#, I have simply made a mistake (unless, perhaps, I am Horowitz). *Adagio* does not tell me precisely what tempo to follow, but if I gallop along like the *William Tell* Overture, instead of winning praise for my interpretation, I will be told that I have got it *wrong*.

Still, I have a Schnabel interpretation of the *Appassionata* Sonata that is two and a half minutes faster than one by Kempff (a difference of about 11 percent), and these two are considered to be among Beethoven's finest interpreters. *The Penguin Guide* gives them both three stars (though only Schnabel gets the rosette). And what shall I say of the most unusual interpretation of Beethoven I have ever heard, this time on FM radio? An accomplished violinist had gotten too old to play the first movement of the violin concerto *(Allegro, ma non troppo)* at a tempo within the normal range. So he played it dramatically slower, creating a difference much greater than that between Schnabel and Kempff. It seemed like a wholly different piece he was playing, and yet, one was reluctant to call his interpretation either mistaken or irresponsible. It threw exhilarating new light on a very familiar composition, and I would prefer to own that recording rather than any number of recordings whose tempi fall within the normal range.

The "open space" we have to traverse between a score and the interpretation we call its performance is such that we can meaningfully call the score a virtual sonata or concerto that only becomes actual in the performance. The same can be said about the relation between the script of a play and its performance. In both cases the phenomenon, to use Wolterstorff's word, radically underdetermines its interpretation. I see no reason why we should not say the same about interpreting texts. This assimilation of reading to performing is implied, I believe, by the account of interpretation Wolterstorff has given to us.

Understood sensibly, such a move carries over to reading the two theses we first encountered with the musical example. First, there is no such thing as *the* interpretation of a text. There will rather be a plurality of differing interpretations deserving of high praise. All will be good interpretations, though none will be *the right* interpretation. Nor should we think that *the right* interpretation is a regulative ideal that performers only approximate, for that would be to assume that the text is in itself fully determinate, an assumption precluded by the concept of interpretation with which we are working.

Second, it will not be the case that interpretation is wholly arbitrary, that anything goes, that all interpretations are equally valid. We are miles from what Wolterstorff calls play-of-interpretations hermeneutics. It will still be possible to get it wrong (e.g., playing F# instead of G#) and to get it right (playing the adagio at a noticeably slower tempo than the *William Tell* Overture). But if, to stick with the musical example, all I succeed in doing is to avoid making such mistakes, I will be so far from giving a good interpretation of the score that I may very well have murdered it. Getting the notes right is one thing; making music is another. Similarly, on the analogy that we are exploring, although there are mistakes to be avoided, giving a good interpretation of a text takes us well beyond getting right what can be gotten right in this fairly straightforward sense, for example, the tense of the verbs.

For some, this latter assurance will not be enough. They feel the need of an objectivity of interpretation that will make it a zero sum game, turning the agony of interpretation into a contest only one can win, the one who comes up with *the right* interpretation. That is what the romantic hermeneutics of authorial intent was all about. If that was not already clear in Schleiermacher, it became abundantly clear in Dilthey, who wanted to preserve the difference between nature and freedom, explanation and understanding, without giving up the ideal of scientifically objective knowledge. Hence the description of his project as a critique of historical reason.

Skepticism and the Quest for Certainty

Here as elsewhere the quest for certainty is the mother of skepticism. The assumption, far more emotional than logical, is that if we do not have

everything, we have nothing; that if we do not have objectivity in interpretation *(the right interpretation)*, we have an anything-goes relativism,
what Wolterstorff calls a play-of-interpretations hermeneutic. Frightened
by sophistry, Platonism makes the unwarranted claim that only its exorbi-
tant claims for human reason can rescue us from those whose rhetorical
skills can make any opinion prevail.

At times it seems that Wolterstorff is wedded to some such objectivism,
one that is incompatible with his own account of interpretation, and that this
objectivism is both part of the motivation and part of the meaning of his
hermeneutics of authorial discourse. Two reasons have emerged for rejecting
the claim that the intent of the author is the meaning of the text, whether that
rejection comes from the philosophical hermeneutics of Gadamer and Ricoeur or from the postmodernism of Foucault, Barthes, and Derrida.[2] The
weak reason, which Wolterstorff accepts, is that it is simply a mistake to
assume that what we are after in interpreting a text is the inner life of the
author, supposedly externalized and made available to us in the text.

The strong reason, which Wolterstorff seems to accept in letter but
not in spirit, is that if, in the spirit of objectivism, we are seeking to close
the gap that I have been calling underdetermination, then appeals to the
intention of the author will not help us. Authors simply do not have the
power to produce texts that will dictate their own interpretation, any more
than composers have the power to compose such scores or playwrights such
scripts. Texts are virtual meanings waiting to be actualized in readings that
will be performances. Reader response criticism and deconstruction jointly
call attention to this indeterminacy of texts; in doing so they point us in
the right direction. What underlies Wolterstorff's critique of Derrida seems
to be the desire to cling to an objectivism that is undermined as much by
his own account of underdetermination as it is by Derrida's account of
différance and undecidability.

In speaking of underdetermination, we are working with a post-Kantian interpretation of interpretation. First, it is Kantian in that every interpretation is the product both of what we receive from and of what we
contribute to the phenomenon being interpreted. But it radicalizes the Kantian insight. Since it is a mistake to assume that our contribution is or should

---

2. For a discussion of these two contexts in which authorial intent is rejected as
the key to a text's meaning, see my essay, "Kierkegaard and the Anxiety of Authorship,"
International Philosophical Quarterly 34 (March 1994): 5-22.

even try to be universally the same from one interpretation to another, interpretation lacks the scientific objectivity that Kant sought to preserve both for Newtonian physics and for our everyday experience of the world.

Wolterstorff stresses that "interpretation is pervasive in human life" and that this fact "reveals something deep and important about the sort of creatures we human beings are." What it reveals about us is that through wide swaths of our experience we are not the kind of critters for whom the epistemological ideals of objectivism are appropriate or for whom the simple either/or between objectivism and subjectivism applies. Things are more open, more pluralistic, more ecumenical than the objectivist assumes; and we need not be afraid to acknowledge this on the assumption that radical, "everything goes" subjectivism is the only alternative. Perhaps God does not need to interpret, but we do. It is part of our finitude.

American evangelicalism has grown out of a fundamentalism that defined itself largely by its difference from Enlightenment modernism. It is ironic that it has been so uncritical of the objectivist assumptions that have fueled the Enlightenment projects of foundationalism, evidentialism, and eventually positivism. (This irony is more general, I think, than the one Wolterstorff points to between evangelicalism and John Locke.) I shall never forget the lecture I heard at an evangelical seminary on the perspicuity of Scripture. A distinguished theologian argued that since the Bible interprets itself, there is no need for us to interpret it. He saw clearly that interpretation is at odds with the objectivism that was as basic to his credo as was his theism — ironically so, since its provenance is not biblical faith but the Enlightenments of ancient Greece and modern Europe.

Wolterstorff is not willing to deny interpretation in this way. But it is not clear that he is willing to draw the full consequences of his own account of the open space presupposed by interpretation, namely, that there is no single correct answer to such questions as "What did Paul say to the Romans?" or "What does God say by appropriating the four Gospels into a Bible that can be called the word of God?"

The Scope of Interpretation

The second question posed above, about the role of interpretation in human life, is in the first instance a question about the scope of interpretation. Wolterstorff speaks of its being "pervasive in human life." How pervasive?

I have mentioned "wide swaths of our experience." How wide? If we think only of those situations in which we set out to interpret something, say, a text, interpretation will surely be less than all pervasive. But for Heidegger and Gadamer that changes the moment we take a comprehensive look at the whole continuum that has deliberate, agonized interpretation at one extreme. Interpretation becomes primordial and all pervasive because all of our judgments about the world, whether we think of them as interpretations or not, presuppose an interpretation or construal of the world, a seeing of the world as such and such a world. Thus, for example, it is not possible to see viruses as causing colds when we have already given an animist construal to the world as a whole.

For Heidegger and Gadamer, one argument for seeing interpretation as foundational in this way (note that interpretation does not preclude argument, and we should expect members of a string quartet, for example, not only to disagree about how to play it, but to give reasons in support of their interpretations) is an argument from analogy. In the classical (i.e., Romantic) theory of text interpretation, the hermeneutical circle is that between part and whole. The interpretation of any part of a text presupposes a prior interpretation of the text as a whole. Thus, if I take the Song of Solomon to be the Hebrew version of the *Kama Sutra,* it is not likely that I will interpret any particular verse as Bernard of Clairvaux does. But the relation is circular in that my readings of parts of a text may lead to changing my readings of the whole, just as anomalies lead to paradigm shifts in science. I may start out by construing *Gulliver's Travels* as a piece of political satire and, after careful study, come to see it as more basically a personal testament of cynical despair.

The analogy simply extends this analysis to the world as a whole. All of our particular judgments about the world presuppose a prior construal of the world in its entirety as this rather than that. Thus Heidegger is able to speak of assertion as a "derivative mode of interpretation."[3] Or, in the language of Kuhnian philosophy of science, all "normal" judgments about the world operate within a "paradigm" that they presuppose and that is itself an interpretation, underdetermined by the world it interprets. Like musical scores and authorial intentions, the world itself (at least in relation to finite knowers like ourselves) is too weak to determine or to dictate its own interpretation. The real world is a virtual reality.

---

3. Martin Heidegger, *Being and Time,* trans. John Macquarrie and Edward Robinson (New York: Harper & Row, 1962), ¶33.

At this point the importance of hermeneutics for a Christian world-view consists of the reminder, first, that all of our judgments are worldview relative and, second, that all worldviews are interpretations and subject to the logic of interpretation. A plurality of interpretations will be deserving of praise, and the objectivist urge to eliminate all but the right interpretation of the world rests on a misunderstanding of who we are. Still, it will not for a moment follow that everything goes or that all worldviews are equally sound.

As developed by Heidegger and Gadamer, the all-pervasive primordiality of interpretation obviously undermines the aspirations of classical foundationalism. If every foundation is an interpretation, then none can have the certainty and finality required by that project. But the all-pervasive primordiality of interpretation is just as unfriendly to any antifoundationalist theory of properly basic beliefs that either denies or ignores the interpretative horizon within which properly basic beliefs occur. (A closer look will reveal that on this account properly basic beliefs are not as "basic" as they seem, but presuppose a world-construal of some sort.)

A somewhat different perspective on the inherently pluralistic character of interpretation derives from Gadamer's notion of *Wirkungs-geschichte*. We return from wholesale to retail interpretation and focus attention on the history of the interpretation of a particular phenomenon such as a text. The *Wirkungsgeschichte* or history of effect of a text is not simply the story of its impact, first in this period and then in that period. The various interpretations of a text, and thus its various "workings" in the world, are in an important sense internal to the text; they belong to its being as completing its being, as giving determinacy to something not fully determinate. Thus the meaning of a text is conceptually inseparable from the history of its interpretation, a history that will be composed of a variety of readings.

These readings will not necessarily be mutually compatible, just as a *rubato* reading of a musical score is not compatible with those readings that eschew *rubato*. In this way a text is unlike Descartes's wax. What Descartes shows is that we cannot determine what the wax is simply by experiencing it in one context. We have to introduce it into a variety of contexts, different temperatures, for example, to get an adequate knowledge of it. But Descartes does not allow this plurality — hard at this temperature, soft at that temperature, and liquid at this temperature — to compromise the objectivism to which he was as deeply wedded as the evangelical Cartesian I mentioned earlier. This context-relative pluralism is immediately designated as appearance rather than reality. It involves the secondary, subjective qualities dependent on the senses, while the intellect is able to surpass them to a fully determinate and fixed essential nature of the wax. For this modern asceticism the body and its senses are to be transcended, not because of their link with sexuality, but because of their link with plurality. Where spirituality once feared the concupiscence of the body, science (and, too often, theology aspiring to be science) now fears its contextuality.

Like Descartes, the notion of *Wirkungsgeschichte* suggests that to interpret a text properly we must take into account the variety of contexts and interpretations that make up its history. But Gadamerian texts are unlike Cartesian wax in that we are not entitled to posit an intellect that can transcend the resultant plurality of meanings to reach an inner essence that is both fully determinate and context free.

Since we are talking about wax, it might be well to ask whether *Wirkungsgeschichte* makes texts, including the biblical text, into wax noses that we can shape any way we like? Perhaps it is a combination of fear and the will to power rather than calm, lucid insight that leads to such a conclusion. While texts may well be too weak to determine their own interpretation single-handedly, they do have a rather remarkable recalcitrance in the presence of arbitrariness. And it may very well be that they effectively resist being taken for Cartesian objects, fully determinate in themselves and open to only a single correct account. If so, the textuality of texts undermines any theology that postulates Enlightenment objectivism as its horizon or paradigm and in that context treats texts, including the biblical text, as wax noses by compelling them to meet the expectations of a philosophical theory that comes to us from Plato and Descartes rather than from Jesus and Paul.

The Truth of the Matter:
Interpretation as Art and Science

Truth, Universality, and Interpretation

DONALD MARSHALL

Wolfhart Pannenberg begins his systematic theology with a provocative question: Why should anyone become a Christian? Though many at present receive Christianity as a heritage from parents and community, the question remains fundamental. It was posed directly to the first Christians and again today in light of our awareness of other religious traditions and of commonplace atheism. Christianity is revelation, which means that it is not conferred on individuals automatically but is a proclamation addressed to their free assent. To become a Christian is to believe that Jesus is Christ, to believe, in Pannenberg's words, "that in [Jesus] God has been active to restore and reconcile the human race and through the human race his entire creation." Why should an individual believe that? For Pannenberg there can only be one answer, a startlingly simple answer: it is true. Precisely because this answer is so simple but has such momentous consequences, we must ask what it means — that is, we must try to understand it fully and deeply. Jesus tells Pilate, "For this I came into the world, to testify to the truth. Everyone who belongs to the truth listens to my voice" (John 18:37). "What is truth?" said a jesting Pilate who would not stay for an answer. We, however, must stay for an answer.

What makes this question compelling for hermeneutics is that for us, Christian revelation is proclamation — what stands written in Scripture. Even for the first witnesses, their belief is an interpretation of the Hebrew Scriptures. When the women found the empty tomb, two men in dazzling apparel asked them why they sought the living among the dead and added, "Remember how he told you" (Luke 24:6) that he must be delivered up and crucified and rise on the third day. "Then they remembered his words" (Luke 24:8). But when they reported to the apostles, "these words seemed to them an idle tale, and they did not believe them" (Luke 24:11). This scene, in which the women believe in light of the words of Jesus that they remember, is followed in Luke's gospel by the two bewildered disciples on the road to Emmaus. Unrecognized, Jesus appeared to them and rebuked their confusion: "Oh, how foolish you are, and how slow of heart to believe all that the prophets have declared" (Luke 24:25). "Then beginning with Moses and all the prophets, he interpreted to them the things about himself in all the scriptures" (Luke 24:27). They only recognized him in the shared meal when he blessed the bread, broke it, and gave it to them. Jesus immediately vanished, but they say to each other, "Were not our hearts burning within us while he was talking to us on the road, while he was opening the scriptures to us?" (Luke 24:32).

Both of these words — *true* and *interpretation* — are difficult for modern ears to hear. To call religious claims "true" disturbs us. Truth is in its nature exclusive, bluntly opposed to the false. It allows no middle ground of opinion on which to negotiate social relations in cases where claims are disputed or disallowed. Truth brings not peace but a sword. Christian and anti-Christian alike fear that the sword will not be metaphorical. In the degrees of holy war stretching from Crusade to mere everyday arrogance, we find no place for humility or taking care not to judge others. Perhaps even more alarming, whatever I admit to be true lays its claim not just against others but against myself. It will be used in evidence against me, just as Socrates' victims concede some point only to discover at the end of a long train of reasoning that they have convicted themselves, like David under the interrogation of Nathan (2 Sam. 12:1-14). And the case is aggravated when "truth" turns out to be an "interpretation" — or, as the revealing phrase goes, "just an interpretation" or even "just your interpretation." Interpretation seems to carry us away from truth, not toward it.

Hence, I think a Christian has to ask this fundamental hermeneutic question: Can truth come to us through an interpretation? This is the question that I am going to address, however inadequately. I will take as a guiding clue Aristotle's discrimination in Book Six of the *Nicomachean*

Ethics[1] of three kinds of knowing through which the mind attains truth: *episteme*, or certain knowledge based on reasoning from sound principles; *techne*, or knowledge shown in the construction of things; and *phronesis*, or knowledge shown in the choice of right actions.

Episteme and the Limits of Knowledge

To begin, I will turn to a work by Aristotle's teacher, Plato, the dialogue called "The Sophist."[2] This dialogue begins from a concern to establish the difference between a sophist and a philosopher. The sophists, in Plato's account, were teachers of rhetoric not bound or loyal to a particular city. For a fee, they offered to teach men how to persuade others, that is, how to get them to see any situation as the speaker wanted them to see it, so that on that basis they would act as he wanted them to act. In contrast, the philosopher seeks only wisdom, what is true in itself for himself and for others, and action faithful to truth. Drawing the difference is, obviously, a problem of definition, but what makes it difficult, Plato remarks, is that the sophists are not passive objects of our stipulations but recognize the polemic intent behind the distinction and consequently dispute every proposed definition and try to evade them all.

The struggle to capture the sophist, to pin him down, comes to center on the argument that the sophist is a manipulator of appearances rather than of truth. But the evasive sophist will reply that if he does not speak truth, then he speaks falsehoods; therefore he speaks what is not; but to speak what is not is to speak nothing; and to say nothing is not to speak at all. Hence, it is not possible not to speak truth. This argument obviously juggles with words. But that is just the point, for we are seeking a definition, words in which to capture the sophist, and we cannot just brush aside the

1. Aristotle, *Nicomachean Ethics*, trans. H. Rackham, rev. ed. (Cambridge: Harvard Univ. Press, 1934). I follow the interpretation of chap. 6 in Hans-Georg Gadamer, *Truth and Method*, 2d rev. ed., trans. Joel Weinsheimer and Donald G. Marshall (New York: Crossroad, 1989), pp. 312-24.

2. Plato, *Theaetetus, Sophist*, trans. Harold North Fowler (Cambridge: Harvard Univ. Press, 1921). For a recent translation, see *The Being of the Beautiful: Plato's Theaetetus, Sophist, and Statesman*, trans. Seth Benardete (Chicago: Univ. of Chicago Press, 1984). My reading is indebted to Stanley Rosen, *Plato's Sophist: The Drama of Original and Image* (New Haven: Yale Univ. Press, 1983).

sophist's words and lay claim to some downright common sense that needs no discussion. In fact, through the sophist's argument we can glimpse a key issue: What is truth? If the truth is what really exists, then how can lies or fictions, which have no truth, exist?

Plato's line of thought is too long and complicated to present fully here. But at its core is the very medium in which the problem has come to light, namely, *logos,* the language of disputation. Plato holds fast to *logos* and uncovers what comes to light in all speaking, namely, a power to bring things together. Through names, a thing rises out of the immediate stream of experience and comes to stand and endure. This standing forth is the moment of truth, the point at which experience becomes susceptible to the conceptual clarification of definition and classification. By pursuing these resources of clarification to their ultimate stopping point, Plato claims to lay bare the most fundamental constituents of intelligible experience. Those constituents are the "five highest genera": being, rest, motion, same, and other.

On reflection, we can see that these terms offer versions of the peculiar little word *is.* We can say simply that something is; we can say that this is that, meaning this is the same as that; or this is not that, meaning this is different from that; or this is here now, and hence at rest; or this is here now and there later, and hence in motion, that is, involved in the process of becoming. It is the interweaving of these five highest genera, reflected in the interweaving of names accomplished by language, *logos,* that connects these most universal forms of reality with the changing world of appearances in which we live directly. I say "reflected" in language, but Plato seems to say something stronger, namely, that language *(logos)* is itself another of these genera,[3] one whose own being consists precisely in enabling the interweaving of the fundamental constituents of everything that exists.[4]

What emerges from this summary of a very intricate argument is the following. Whenever something rises out of the flow of experience and comes to stand and endure, as it does preeminently when we give it a name, we enter onto a possible path of conceptual clarification through definition and categorization that leads us eventually to the ultimate constituents not just of our words but of reality. This entire structure, sustained and rendered

---

3. Plato, *Sophist,* 260A.

4. My interpretation here reflects Paul Friedländer, *Plato,* trans. Hans Meyerhoff, 3 vols. (New York: Pantheon, 1958-69), 3:277.

concrete in *logos*, constitutes the truth of everything that is. Since it is a rigorous and demonstrative truth attained through dialectic, it yields for us *episteme*, knowledge in the emphatic sense and of the fully theoretical sort that Aristotle is pointing to.

This conception of knowledge and of the truth to be sought has certainly influenced both Christian theology and literary interpretation more generally. Historically, we can see the issue emerge in the transition from *lectio divina*, the thoughtful reading of Scripture, to dialectic disputations on doctrinal matters issuing into rationally structured compendia called *summae*. Bernard of Clairvaux (1090–1153), for example, reportedly "read frequently and in order through the canonical scriptures, with no intention beyond the straightforward one of understanding them."[5] Such slow reading, "ruminating" over the text, issues in sermons that essentially rewrite the texts of Scripture and the fathers who have commented on them. Any puzzles or difficulties that arise are resolved not by logical methods, but by Scripture itself, its context or higher meanings (e.g., the overarching meaning of "charity," which Augustine in his *On Christian Doctrine* specifies as the *res* or substance of Scripture with which the interpretation of any passage must harmonize).[6] The aim is practical, the transformation of the preacher's own character and that of the auditors, so that faith is strengthened.

Bernard's great enemy was Peter Abelard (1079–1142), who expressed open contempt for the inability of those who merely wrote glosses on Scripture to answer any very penetrating doctrinal question that arose in the course of their commentaries. Moved by an appreciation of Aristotelian logic that bore fruit in Scholasticism, instead of following the narrative sequence of Scripture he collected passages around questions, particularly focused on contradictions. The effect, whether fully intended or not, was to displace Scripture from the center of sacred study and turn theology into a set of problems resolved dialectically, not hermeneutically. Abelard wanted to replace mere words, even the words of Scripture, with reasons that would

---

5. William of St. Thierry, *Sancti Bernadi: Vita et Res Gestae* I PL 185.241A-B, cited by Eileen Sweeney, "Rewriting the Narrative of Scripture: Twelfth-Century Debates Over Reason and Theological Form," *Medieval Philosophy and Theology* 3 (1993): 1-34. My comments on Bernard and Abelard are drawn from this article.

6. St. Augustine, *On Christian Doctrine*, trans. D. W. Robertson (Indianapolis: Bobbs-Merrill, 1958). The discussion takes up Book I.

be humanly and logically intelligible. He wanted words to carry their meanings with them, not to initiate a temporal and inevitably partial process of
seeking meaning. But when Bernard engineered Abelard's condemnation
at the Council of Sens in 1141, he accused Abelard of undermining faith,
and the condemnation contributed to congealing a supposed opposition
between reason and faith that has had fateful consequences.

A similar fate befalls not the doctrinal but the moral content of
Scripture. This is clear in Benedict de Spinoza's *Theologico-Political Treatise*.
Spinoza argues that God reveals himself to the prophets in forms — words
and images — suited to their vivid imaginations and individual personalities. The prophets' discourses, in turn, are adapted to the understandings
and imaginations of common people, to stir up their devotion and to draw
their obedience. But reliable insight into spiritual and moral matters can
only be attained through the light of reason. Spinoza thus splits Scripture
sharply into two parts. On the one side, using our own reason, we can
perceive the moral precepts in Scripture, which "are expressed in very
ordinary language, and are equally simple and easily understood."[7] Everything else — the imagery, narratives, laws, ceremonies, and so on — simply
reflects the specific imaginations and historical circumstances of their
authors and audiences and has no authority whatever over those in other
circumstances. Scripture ceases to be the ground of moral insight; instead,
moral insights derived directly from reason provide a standard against
which to judge Scripture and to decide which parts are true and which are
merely products of their times.

While literary works do not lay the same claim as Scripture to doctrinal authority, they too can be approached in the spirit of conceptual rationality. This is exactly Plato's approach to tragedy and epic in Book Three
of the *Republic*, where he extracts the lesson about the nature of the gods
or the standards of human conduct that various traditional Greek tales are
taken to exemplify and then condemns those lessons for being opposed to
what reason discloses as truth. Plato notes that some critics have developed
techniques of allegorical interpretation that save the tales by subordinating
them to more acceptable ideas. And, in fact, from antiquity to the present,
critics drawing on systems of thought from neoplatonic philosophy to
psychoanalysis tease out of literary works meanings sometimes plausible,

7. Benedict de Spinoza, *A Theologico-Political Treatise*, trans. R. H. M. Elwes (New
York: Dover, 1951), p. 113.

sometimes far-fetched, touching on metaphysical doctrines, moral principles, or human psychology. These approaches have in common that they bring to the text substantive ideas and a conception of sound reasoning that precede reading and cannot be affected by it.

Literary interpretation adds one opportunity for the subordination of the work to a rational scheme that biblical interpretation precludes, namely, the subordination of the work's form to rules of formal construction that may be arrived at by induction from agreed upon masterpieces but are then validated by an exercise of pure reason. Thus, for example, great tragedies exhibit a concentration of feeling that often expresses itself in an action confined to a short period of time. This inductive generalization can then be rigidified by reason into the rule of the "unity of time," namely, the assertion that a tragic plot must take up no more than twenty-four hours.[8] This rule may then be applied rigidly to condemn some of the very masterpieces on whose authority it was inductively established. The substantive authority of Scripture rules out this kind of mere aesthetic judgment of its form, but it is worth recalling that St. Augustine himself was held back from a commitment to Christianity because Scripture did not meet the formal standards he had assimilated from his study of rhetoric.[9]

A good deal ought to be conceded to the claims of conceptual rationality. A text's meaning cannot be completely unintelligible to us and still be meaning. Even hermetic literature, ancient and modern, which seems to have been crafted to resist intelligibility, preserves intelligibility through its precise resistance to particular forms of it. All speaking entails conceptual presuppositions in its content and in its form as communication, and these can always be traced back to what Kenneth Burke calls "god-terms" and Richard Weaver calls "ultimate terms."[10]

Nevertheless, Aristotle's distinctions are intended to show that various forms of intelligibility can legitimately claim to be rational. If truth is to

---

8. In "A Dialogue on Poetic Drama," prefixed to an edition of John Dryden's *Of Dramatic Poesie: An Essay*, T. S. Eliot offers this interpretation of the "unities." See Joan C. Grace, *Tragic Theory in the Critical Works of Thomas Rymer, John Dennis, and John Dryden* (Rutherford, N.J.: Fairleigh Dickinson Univ. Press, 1975), p. 103.

9. St. Augustine, *Confessions*, trans. William Watts (Cambridge: Harvard, 1912), Book III, Chapter V.

10. See Kenneth Burke, *A Rhetoric of Motives* (Berkeley: Univ. of California Press, 1969), pp. 298-301; for Weaver, see the final chapter of *The Ethics of Rhetoric* (Chicago: Regnery, 1953).

come to us through interpretation, conceptual rationality cannot be what we are seeking. In the turn to reflection here, we are no longer listening to the text but making it the mere occasion to reiterate what we have legitimated on other grounds. Where the text resists this imposition, it will be condemned or ignored, but that collapse of interpretation calls into question not the text but the attempt to control it in this way. The text's concreteness must not be dissipated in some Hegelian sublation into philosophical knowledge.

Techne: Knowledge as Control

Aristotle's second kind of knowledge, *techne,* is the knowledge embedded in our active shaping and making of the material world. From this point of view it is possible to criticize conceptual rationality as merely theoretical. In the *Republic,* Plato says that the carpenter looks to the singular idea of a couch when he makes an actual couch; but Aristotle comments drily that beds are made not with ideas, but by carpenters out of wood using hammers and saws.[11] Aristotle's examples of *techne* are various human crafts, and Francis Bacon's esteem for the practical knowledge of traders, explorers, merchants, and craftsmen leads us to the dawn of modern science.

In making this transition, I do not mean to restrict science to its technological applications. Undoubtedly the serious scientist is motivated by a pure desire to discover the truth of natural processes in and for itself. Nevertheless, the fact that scientific knowledge pursued for itself has repeatedly yielded unexpected and often spectacular technological advances is not accidental but shows something fundamental about this kind of knowing. It is grounded on understanding objects or phenomena as necessarily produced by a precisely specified articulation of matter and forces. Science is not simply a collection of facts and observations nor even a set of accurate predictions. That something is the case or that a prediction comes true counts for nothing in itself. The force of calling a scientific finding "fact" lies not in the fact itself, but in the explanation that exhibits its necessity. Likewise, science is confirmed by the accuracy of predictions

---

11. Plato, *Republic,* trans. Paul Shorey, 2 vols. (Cambridge: Harvard Univ. Press, 1937), Book 10, 596B. I am interpreting Aristotle's objection in *Metaphysics,* trans. Hippocrates G. Apostle (Bloomington: Indiana Univ. Press, 1966), Book A, 991b5-9.

only when those predictions emerge from explanatory mechanisms consistent with scientific method. The science — the knowledge of truth — lies in the explanation.

It is important to see the difference between this kind of explanation, which specifies mechanisms, even when it leads to the formulation of general laws, and the dialectical reasoning described earlier, which subordinates particulars under the constitutive categories of their intelligible being. When physicists explain the material world, their analyses terminate in strange objects, like quarks or Higgs bosons, but not in the dialectic categories of being, same, other, rest, and motion. When Aristotle talks in the *Poetics* about the making of tragedies, a closer look shows that he is specifying the principles — the parts and their interrelations — that rational analysis of the idea of a tragedy requires. This is distinguishable from his scientific way of talking when he speaks as though the tragedian first conceives the specific emotional and intellectual response he wants to produce in the audience and then deploys as means the physical resources of dramatic production that his art assures him will produce that response.[12]

I point to Aristotle's discussion of tragedy here because at first the scientific study of natural processes may seem to have nothing to do with understanding Scripture or literary works. The success of modern science, even more than the claims of conceptual reason, may seem to have rendered obsolete, even slightly ludicrous, the notion that any truth at all could be established on the basis of interpreting texts. It is easy to think of cases where, for example, what Scripture says seems inconsistent with what scientific investigation has established. In fact, however, the most striking effect of the emergence of science has not been to eliminate interest in texts but instead to foster a new way of talking about them. This was already evident in Spinoza. Abandoning the claim of Scripture to universal truth did not have solely negative and destructive consequences. Positively, it meant that the books of the Bible were now freed to be studied in relation to the specific historical circumstances of their creation. Similarly, in the seventeenth-century *querelle des anciens et modernes*, advocates of a modern scientific rationality battled defenders of the superiority of the Greco-Roman classics and abandoned the claim that only studying the classics could nurture the good taste that marked the gentleman. But this liberation of the classics from their moral and pedagogic function paved the way to historical studies

12. Aristotle, *Poetics* (Cambridge: Harvard Univ. Press, 1932).

that generated much more precise and reliable knowledge about antiquity, ancient languages, and ancient texts. It is true that nineteenth-century "higher criticism" of the Bible often felt and often was destructive of acceptance of the authority of Scripture, but to it we also owe a vast body of information about the text of Scripture, the archaeology and history of the Near East, and the historical variety of religious ideas among the Jews.

Closely parallel is the rise of the historical study of literary works. There is considerable distance between Richard Hurd's eighteenth-century presentation of Spenser's *Faerie Queene* against the background of medieval chivalry and its politically motivated revival under Queen Elizabeth, and the elaborated models of the evolution of literary forms inspired by Darwinian theories or the Marxist unmasking of literature as a means for the dominant class to legitimate its self-interest by reflecting all of life in a distorting mirror whose images flattered that class.[13] The conception of literature as the product of its time — not the product of a conscious *techne* on the part of the artist but as a phenomenon to be explained like other natural facts as the outcome of forces and causes operating without any consciousness — such a conception in the hands of a narrow nationalist may turn literature into a testament to some allegedly authentic and unique spirit of a nation or folk. But the other side of the coin is the power of this idea — that literature is a product of its time — to dissolve the bewitching authority of a literary work by laying bare the machine in the ghost.[14]

Despite the achievements of historical and philological research, scientific knowledge is not what we are seeking in understanding Scripture or literary texts. In historical research on the truth of Scripture or the historical forces that produce a text, we lose sight of the real subject. As Wittgenstein says, even indubitability is not enough in the case of religious belief. "Even if there is as much evidence as for Napoleon . . . the indubitability wouldn't be enough to make me change my whole life."[15] That in Scripture which is momentous for our life and fate cannot be reduced to a matter to be decided by experts behind our back, so to speak. The protest

---

13. Richard Hurd, in *Letters on Chivalry and Romance,* ed. Hoyt Trobridge (Los Angeles: Williams Andrews Clark Memorial Library, Univ. of California, 1963).

14. See Geoffrey Hartman, *Beyond Formalism: Literary Essays 1958–1970* (New Haven: Yale Univ. Press, 1970), pp. 356-86.

15. Ludwig Wittgenstein, *Lectures and Conversations on Aesthetics, Psychology and Religious Belief,* ed. Cyril Barrett (Berkeley: Univ. of California Press, 1966), p. 57.

against this kind of "expertise" is not just anti-intellectualism but distrust of the expert who has lost the sense of the real through his methodical objectifications.[16] The apparent contradictions at the level of factual detail have undoubtedly disturbed many believers, but, I think, unnecessarily. On the contrary, they may actually point our attention in the right direction. If the book of Genesis is not a textbook of geology or paleontology, we may be more open to a more important matter, namely, understanding the story of creation as bearing on our relations to each other within a world and human community related to God as his creation. To be sure, common sense loses its own legitimacy and makes itself ridiculous when it pretends to dictate limits to scientific research or ventures opinions about what can be decided only on scientific grounds. On the other side, scientists likewise lose their own legitimacy when an unacknowledged agenda moves them to assert conclusions where evidence is irreparably lacking. Between the researcher and the believer, both struggling to gain the upper hand, lies an area of indeterminacy and free judgment that can never be eliminated.

Phronesis and the Art of Understanding

Aristotle's third category of knowing is *phronesis*, or moral reasoning. In this conception, Aristotle is trying to mediate between the particulars of our action and the principles that ground and justify them. That we are dealing here with a truth that can lay claim to rationality is confirmed by its parallel to Aristotle's account of action.[17] Aristotle draws a parallel between reasoning in matter of theoretical knowledge and reasoning in matters of action. Neither is reducible to the other, but both are rational.[18] In the *Nicomachean Ethics*, he argues that when I choose to do something, my goal and the means to achieve it emerge from deliberation about what I desire and what lies in my power.[19] The reasoning that leads to action,

16. Hans-Georg Gadamer, "The Limitations of the Expert," in *Hans-Georg Gadamer on Education, Poetry, and History: Applied Hermeneutics,* ed. Dieter Misgeld and Graeme Nicholson, trans. Lawrence Schmidt and Monica Reuss (Albany: State Univ. of New York Press, 1992), pp. 181-92.

17. I am following Martha Nussbaum's interpretation of Aristotle in *Aristotle's De Muto Animalia* (Princeton: Princeton Univ. Press, 1978).

18. Nussbaum, *Aristotle's De Motu Animalia,* p. 182.

19. Aristotle, *Nicomachean Ethics,* 3.2-3; 1111b, 1113a.

called a "practical syllogism," holds in structured relation desire, belief, and action.[20] It thus links my perception of what is good with the perception of means to achieve it that are possible for me. The conception of the good articulates my conception of human nature and of the components of the good life for a human being so conceived. This is not abstract theoretical reasoning about the good but an understanding operative concretely within my own desires and actions.[21]

What is the nature of this guiding belief about the good? What makes practical reasoning distinctive is that in this case the particularity of moral action in specific cases is not sacrificed to a general proposition. If I think of formulating the good I aim at as a rule for my behavior, that rule arises from my previous experience and is open to revision in the light of the particular action required of me or in the light of further experience. This is why Aristotle insists on equity, which corrects rules when their application would be unjust or unreasonable. As Martha Nussbaum puts it, "our ultimate responsibility is the complexities of the particular." Moreover, such rules are in their nature "indefinite."[22] Moral rules are outlines or sketches, and adopting them means taking responsibility to fill them out in my specific actions.[23]

For my action to be moral, I must take thought to formulate its ground. But to call this formulation a "rule" misleads us into expecting it to be defined precisely and structured into a system of rules. Aristotle instead speaks of *phantasmata*, "images." These are not simply passively received pictures of the world, but representations actively formed by the thinking, rational, discursive mind.[24] In short, they are interpretations formed by the individual or taken over from the repertory stored up in his culture. Part of Aristotle's conception is that images formed in this way may enable us to perceive "things, structures and relationships of which we had previously been unaware."[25] This is the point of his famous remark in the *Poetics* that tragedy is more philosophical than history, because it expresses

20. Nussbaum, *Aristotle's De Motu Animalia*, p. 188.

21. Nussbaum, *Aristotle's De Motu Animalia*, pp. 195-96.

22. Nussbaum, *Aristotle's De Motu Animalia*, pp. 213-14. Aristotle, *Nichomachean Ethics*, 1137b29.

23. Aristotle, *Nichomachean Ethics*, 1104a1-2.

24. Aristotle, *Motion of Animals*, 433b31-434a10; Nussbaum, *Aristotle's De Motu Animalia*, p. 234.

25. Nussbaum, *Aristotle's De Motu Animalia*, p. 227.

the universal.[26] He means that the coherent image of human action discursively constructed in a tragedy's plot enables us to hold it before the mind and contemplate it, with the result that we gain insights that are applicable in our experience beyond the specific actions presented in the play.

This is true even if the represented actions are entirely fictional, though we feel our insights are more reliable if they are anchored in real events. By "universal," Aristotle explains that he means that tragedy shows the kind of thing a certain kind of person may do or say, but this apparently theoretical notion of "kind" is further explicated when he urges the playwright to begin by grasping his plot in outline as a "universal," that is, "as a whole."[27] He means that each moment in the plot should follow from what immediately precedes it and lead into what immediately follows, and that the whole should connect beginning to end through an unbroken chain of mediating links. The universal here does not arise from a dialectic that abandons the particular in pursuit of an ultimate theoretical term, nor in a scientific objectification that uncovers the causal law mechanically governing action. It lies instead in the power of a coherent narrative to show the practical reasons why a considerable person succeeded or failed in living a good life.

Despite the illuminating relevance of Aristotle's conception of the role of *phantasmata* in practical reasoning, we must look elsewhere for conceptions that bring out some further elements of interpretation. For practical reasoning is still too local and self-sufficient to express the strongest claim of interpretation to universality. We can supplement Aristotle's theory with Erich Auerbach's account of the technique for interpreting Scripture that the early Church Fathers called "figura." Already in Paul's epistles, events in the Hebrew Scriptures are seen as prefigurations of events in the life of Christ.[28] To take a famous later example from Dante, the Israelites crossing the Red Sea are a figure of Christ's crucifixion. For Paul, through figural interpretation the Old Testament ceased to be a revelation of law and a historical record of God's dealings with Israel and became instead a prefiguration of Christ, whose message is to Jew and Gentile alike. The reality of the Old Testament record

---

26. Aristotle, *Poetics*, 9:1451b6-7.

27. Aristotle, *Poetics*, 17:1455b1.

28. Erich Auerbach, "Figura," in *Scenes from the Drama of European Literature* (New York: Meridian, 1959), pp. 9-76.

is not denied, nor is it translated, as Philo did in his Platonizing allegorical interpretations, into conceptual terms. But it gains the character of promise directed toward a future unknown to those who spoke and acted in it. "In this light," Auerbach says, "the history of no epoch ever has the practical self-sufficiency which, from the standpoint both of primitive man and of modern science, resides in the accomplished fact; all history, rather, remains open and questionable, points to something still concealed."[29] As figural interpretation developed, scriptural events were related not only to the life of Christ but to the life of the individual believer (who is exhorted to imitate Christ) and ultimately to eschatological fulfillment in the final judgment of God, when the meaning of the whole of history will be revealed and consummated. The interpretive process in which understanding of what comes to appear in texts is fulfilled in our present action thus gains a new depth. For our action in the light of what is revealed through texts both fulfills the promise they are understood to contain and itself constitutes a new promise awaiting further and ultimate fulfillment.

The vocation of truth requires that we mediate the relation of everyday life to the two great constructive powers of reason and modern science.[30] This task requires that whatever we think about must be withdrawn from immediate experience, brought to stand, and examined and tested. Reason and science assert the indispensability of a critical distance that liberates us from the domination of the immediate and the particular. To say that a text speaks to us means that it does not allow us to push it away critically and judge it in our own terms. And yet everything put into language and even more into written language has already effected this withdrawal and bringing to stand. Interpreting what is written has its own vocation, namely, to stay with what comes to view in language, not to dissolve it into objectifications. The power of interpretive consciousness lies in grasping a question — not a question we put critically to a text, but the question the text puts to us. A text that puts us to the question separates us from our mere desires and wishes, from the commitments and entanglements of our present course of life.

A question may be answered yes or no, but opening that choice does not dissolve the authority of the text. Instead, it brings that authority to

---

29. Auerbach, "Figura," p. 58.

30. This paragraph is indebted for ideas and phrasing to Hans-Georg Gadamer, *Philosophical Hermeneutics*, trans. David E. Linge (Berkeley: Univ. of California Press, 1976).

bear most sharply against its reader. The validity of the question lies in the reader's freely accepted responsibility to respond, to be answerable for the answer given. The interpreter's capacity to stay with the meaning of a text aims not at blind submission but at intelligent assent.[31] Understanding makes what is alien our own. Interpretation arises when one confronts a tradition to which one has never belonged or which one no longer unquestioningly accepts. The interpreter's answer to the question the text poses enables the text to speak again into a present situation. The text's reality lies in our keeping it alive, in "testifying" or "witnessing" its truth through our own actions. Where understanding means assuming responsibility to make the text speak again with power to affect present action, interpretation has the character of an event.

The claim to truth and hence to universality of the interpreter's answer to the text does not lie in the self-closure of reflective reason nor in the fashioning of an explanation that liberates itself from the contingencies of time and space. It lies instead in the openness of action to a future where it will have consequences and serve as the material of further interpretation. In specifically linguistic terms, this openness resides in an interpretation's address to other people, inviting them to test and validate its truth through their own interpretive acts. This is to recognize, in Lesslie Newbigin's pungent phrase, "the Congregation as hermeneutic of the Gospel."[32] It is what Josiah Royce described as an "interpretive community" in his powerful book *The Problem of Christianity*.[33] The universality

31. In two important essays, Gadamer argues that truth must always be understood as an adequate answer to a genuine, serious question. This means that we cannot understand what is stated in a text without grasping correctly the question that statement answers. Both the answer and the question can be sophistic, misleading, ill-formulated, or the like. But the relation of a propositional statement to a given reality must always pass through a recognition of the question to which the proposition responds. On really important matters, an answer may seem quite narrowly focused, but through the question behind it, it may implicate the whole of our existence. See "Truth in the Human Sciences" and "What Is Truth?" in *Hermeneutics and Truth*, ed. Brice R. Wachterhauser (Evanston, Ill.: Northwestern Univ. Press, 1994), pp. 25-32 and 33-46, respectively.

32. Lesslie Newbigin, *The Gospel in a Pluralist Society* (Grand Rapids: Eerdmans, 1989), pp. 222-33.

33. I have discussed some implications of Royce's ideas for literary interpretation in "Reading and Interpretive Communities," in *The Discerning Reader*, ed. David Barratt, Roger Pooley, and Leland Ryken (Leicester: Inter-Varsity Press, 1995), pp. 69-84, esp. 79-84.

of interpretation has the form of openness to endless dialogue. What is universal about interpretation is that it looks for confirmation in further experience, including the experience of others, and hence it must be published, brought into the life not only of a particular community but of all humankind.[34] The fact that Christianity is a question each must answer for himself or herself does not mean isolation. On the contrary, the answer comes in language, and speaking a language presupposes that one already stands in a community, even if the answer so challenges that existing community as to call for the emergence of another. The medium in which the promise of any text is fulfilled is not just the individual life but the lives of all those bound together in the interpretive process that stretches from the first revelation of the text to the end of time. We thus return to our starting point, the question "Why become a Christian?" The answer must be that we choose to join the community that by its actions asserts and takes responsibility for the truth that comes to it through the word of Scripture.

---

34. Newbigin, *Gospel in a Pluralist Society*, pp. 35, 77, 126.

Cure of Body and Soul:
Intepretation as Art and Science[1]

ELLEN T. CHARRY

Interpretation has a practical goal: to transform the preacher's character and strengthen the audience's faith by engaging the Christian drama. The question is, What truth can the process of interpretation claim in the face of scientific claims that truth is that which can be quantified, predicted, or explained? For while transformation of the preacher and audience is desired, it cannot be predicted or quantified. That is the work of the Holy Spirit. Donald Marshall's argument takes the form of backing off from claiming that Christian interpretation is a science to claiming that interpretation is an act of conceptual clarification like that of other literary interpretation, because it is a field from which "indeterminacy and free judgment can never be eliminated."

I hope to strengthen Marshall's claim about the truth of interpretation with some observations about the distinction he draws between *techne* and *phronesis*, between skill and wisdom, or as he treats them, science and art. Marshall, like most modern Christian interpreters, has been unnecessarily diffident in his claim for a purely artistic truth of interpretation. Theology has stronger epistemic ground to stand on than theologians have recently claimed.

Marshall's argument for understanding the religious interpretation of texts rests on a rather clear distinction between science and interpretation that has to do with engagement. Science requires rigorous distance between

1. Excerpted from Chapter 1 of *"By the Renewing of Your Minds": The Salutarity of Christian Doctrine* (New York: Oxford Univ. Press, 1997). Copyright Ellen Charry.

the investigator and the object under investigation, so that the knower is eliminated as a factor in the production of knowledge and so that all knowers will know the same things of the object to be known. Interpretation of texts, the primary task of theology, on the other hand, does not admit of the distance between the knower and the known. As Hans-Georg Gadamer has pointed out, the interpreter brings her whole self, social and emotional, to the text.[2] Under the rules guiding *techne,* the engagement of the knower with the thing to be known disqualifies theology as a science. The canons of scientific method that require objectivity render theological hermeneutics an art rather than a science. This is by now a common view of the situation, which theologians take to suggest that what they do lacks scientific punch. Donald Marshall has framed the issue much as liberal Protestantism has: Genesis is not a science book, but it may be a good text for studying human relations.

Marshall has helpfully pointed out a happy side effect of this circumstance, one often omitted by the objectivity-seeking academic guilds that rush to be as scientific and value-free as possible. The consequence is that the interpreter, unlike the scientist, is able to hold values, to offer edifying interpretations that are immediately practical and that intend to form their readers. Indeed, were this not the case, it would be difficult to grasp the benefit of the interpretive process for reading communities that seek to be guided by such texts. The difference between scientists and theologians, then, is that scientists are unable or unwilling to make normative recommendations regarding the use of their findings, while theologians commend their readings of texts based on the commitments of the tradition within which they stand as interpreters.

I am in sympathy with the Gadamerian perspective and its practical implications. Yet, while familiar with the distinction between objective science and interpretation that requires wisdom, I have become less willing to cede so much ground to the number crunchers, and fear that religious types have retreated too hastily into a defensive posture vis-à-vis hard science. This is to say that interpretation and science are not necessarily always in opposition. Every statistician knows how much power resides in the hands of the interpreter. We need to fuzz the distinction Marshall has drawn between *techne* and *phronesis* so that moral reasoning may lay claim to a stronger basis than that which comes from standing within a commu-

---

2. See Hans-Georg Gadamer, *Truth and Method,* 2nd rev. ed., trans. Joel Weinsheimer and Donald G. Marshall (New York: Crossroad, 1989).

nity of interpreters only. Moral reasoning, I will argue, may lay claim to truth because it produces results.

Science is not monolithic. There are different models of science, some more hard core than others. Some do rely purely on the experimental method of repeatability and predictability; but not all do exclusively. Yet diffident religious types generally take as disciplinary standards for themselves only the harder forms of reason and science, those that allow no room for the type of moral and practical reasoning that theological knowledge claims to represent. There is, however, a "kinder, gentler" scientific reasoning on whose terms Christian truth and knowledge might be emboldened.

I have in mind a soft or weak rationalism that employs conceptual clarity, technical knowledge, and concrete interpretation. Some forms of scientific reasoning require interpretive moves that rely on wisdom precisely as a set of skills that constitutes science as an art. As such, it has more in common with hermeneutics than has generally been recognized: engagement between the knower and the known, embeddedness in the immediate particulars of the situation, and development of a set of competencies akin to the knowledge competency required of the interpreter.

Another way of putting the point is to suggest that some forms of science, notably clinical forms such as interpretation, are arts. They are not autonomous or mechanistic, such that if one follows the rules or runs the data through a computer the expected results will inevitably emerge. Specifically, clinical medicine is such an art. It requires discerning judgment, the involvement of the doctor and the patient with one another, and the employment of scientific knowledge. Clinical medical practice is as much an art as is theology, and theological interpretation is as much a science as is medicine.

The medical model, in brief, is an epistemic tool that one can use to argue that theology and the interpretive task are best understood not as theoretical sciences but as practical sciences whose goal is not simply conceptual clarity but, as Marshall all but suggests, the cure of souls.

The goal here is to present a case for what Janet Soskice calls a cautious critical theological realism, the position that theological terms are not "logical ciphers but . . . terms which putatively refer to possibly real entities, relations, and states of affairs."[3] On this view, the art of Christian practice

3. Janet Martin Soskice, "Theological Realism," in *The Rationality of Religious Belief*, ed. William J. Abraham and Steven W. Holtzer (Oxford: Clarendon Press, 1987), pp. 105-19.

may make a stronger claim to truth than that resting on the common language of a community of interpreters. It will certainly do that but it will also make a claim to knowledge that transcends the interpretive community. In short, *techne* and *phronesis*, while they may be logically distinct categories, are required in both clinical medicine and theology. Over the past three hundred years, theology has been so insecure about its identity vis-à-vis hard science that it has either let go of its legitimate vocation to practical wisdom and focused exclusively on conceptual clarity to compete with science, or it has so burrowed itself in the subjective interpretive task that it has backed off from making truth claims altogether.

Medicine and Theology: The Hermeneutical Analogies

There are pointed similarities between the power of medicine to cure physical ailments and the power of interpretation to strengthen Christian faith. As noted, both are clinical disciplines that require sound knowledge of basic principles, careful judgment of a total situation, including inference and the interpretation of data, and cooperative trust among the parties involved. Both arts must be applied with care and caution in every circumstance. Neither is a lockstep process that proceeds of its own accord.

First, medicine, like interpretation, requires knowledge. It relies upon knowledge of the body and the processes of health and disease, of diagnostic procedures, and of the many effects of medications. Theology also requires knowledge. It relies upon knowledge of the doctrines of the faith and how they are understood to effect spiritual healing, of theological anthropology, and of the social and intellectual setting in which theological interpretation is made.

One might object that we have better knowledge of the workings of health and disease than we do of God's work of salvation. I do not consider this objection a strong one, as there are many diseases we do not understand and others that we cannot treat. In fact, there might be support for the view that spiritual deformity in the form of sin is better understood than are some diseases, and that therapy for it is more readily available. The fact that various Christian traditions understand the process of spiritual healing differently — Catholics rely more on the sacramental power of the church, while Protestants rely more on the power of the word of God — should not lessen support for this view. Medicine also employs a variety of treatment modalities, and judging among them requires careful discernment, as well as attention to their application in any given setting.

Success in medicine and theology also requires highly skilled judgment and interpretation of clinical data based on the latest knowledge at hand. Competent medical practice requires initial careful judgment and continuous reassessment on the part of the physician and other health-care workers. Health-care workers must ask the right questions of the patient — who must supply the right answers — in order to render a diagnosis and to construct a treatment plan appropriate to the patient's situation and resources. Clinical judgment has guided medical practice for centuries. With the use of advanced technology in diagnosis and treatment, such judgment may be less visible. That is the case, not because judgment is less reliable now that we have more precise diagnostic tools, but because the litigious mood of contemporary society requires physicians to protect themselves. Indeed, clinical judgment may be preferred over empirical diagnostic tests that may prove false or misleading. Physicians may need to reassess the treatment that they recommend and be ready to adjust or change a course of therapy and determine when it is complete or ineffective.

Theological practice also relies on careful assessment of available knowledge. While there is a standard set of core Christian doctrines that unite Christian traditions, the interpretation of them is very broad. East and West agree on the triune identity of God, but they disagree on the *filioque*. While the West pinpoints the cross as the locus of salvation, the East stresses the resurrection. Catholics highlight the incarnation, while Protestants emphasize justification. Employing these doctrines in the cause of spiritual and moral healing requires the same degree of judgment by the skilled practitioner, the theologian or pastor, within the known body of theological knowledge.

Recently, there has been renewed attention to the use of cumulative case arguments in philosophy of religion.[4] In contrast to a formal chain of deductive reasoning to demonstrate the a priori existence of God, reliance on informed judgment is again being recognized as a legitimate form of reasoning in building a case for theistic belief. Cumulative case arguments evaluate a series of considerations based on available evidence to arrive at a reasoned conviction. While this may be jarring to those schooled on

4. See Abraham and Holtzer, eds., *Rationality of Religious Belief;* and Basil Mitchell, *The Justification of Religious Belief* (New York: Seabury, 1974).

deductive reasoning in philosophy of religion, it should come as no surprise to those who accept inductive reasoning and interpretation of evidence in the practice of medicine.

Clinical pharmacology employs inferential reasoning that illuminates the parallel between theology and medicine. As should be evident by now, the use of medication is but one, albeit powerful, part of successful medical treatment. Many conditions are controlled not with or not only with medication but with proper diet, exercise, surgery, or simply palliation in cases in which no treatment is available, including the common cold. Nevertheless, medication is essential in many cases. The general public rarely realizes that the action of many medications is poorly understood or unknown.[5]

New medications are mostly discovered by tedious processes of trial and error, or accident. Placebos are effective on occasion, but their effectiveness depends more on trust in the physician than on pharmacological action. That is, there is a degree of mystery in the pharmacology of many medications; their authorization for use by the Food and Drug Administration is based on success in clinical trials rather than on an objective demonstration of their action in a research laboratory. Drugs that work in the laboratory may fail in clinical trials. For that reason, drugs are trusted and prescribed on the basis of their demonstrated effects, not their theoretical cogency.

The situation in medicine goes to the heart of David Hume's criticism of inference in theology. Hume argued that those things that we take to be the effects of God's work do not yield sure knowledge of God, or indeed any knowledge at all. But he may have made an overhasty judgment. The fact that Christian faith and practice do transform believers' lives parallels the medical evidence that a medication may be effective against an illness regardless of how well either the mechanism of the disease or the medication is understood.

Soskice has argued that models in theology, like those in science, are intentionally constructed and subsequently modified with further research and understanding, especially in the face of clinical trials. Theology has a theoretical component, including standardized language to describe the

---

5. E.g., the actions of Wellbutrin and Ludiomil, used to treat depression, are unknown, and the actions of Blenoxane and Megace, palliatives to treat carcinoma, are poorly known, as is Ritalin, used to treat children with attention deficit disorders, and Esidrix, used to fight hypertension.

Person of Christ and the Trinity. But it is the experience of faith or sanctification that provides crucial evidence for the adequacy of these theories and the possible need for their adjustment. Just as poorly understood medications are prescribed based on clinical evidence, the power of God to effect spiritual transformation is trusted by Christians even though human language expressing the reality of God, like the action of the drug, remains elusive and may later call for modification.[6] In this sense, clinical medicine and theology both employ a soft rationalism whose findings are reliable even if later they need to be adjusted in light of subsequent cases or experience.[7]

The third and final analogy between medical and theological arts is the requirement of trust and obedience. Although a patient will rarely have as much medical knowledge as does the physician, the patient bears a degree of responsibility for her own treatment, beginning with knowing when to seek medical help. To be treated successfully patients must trust the caregivers and obey the course of therapy. Abuse of medication, diet, or exercise, or failure to persevere with a course of treatment will thwart the finest medical efforts. At the same time, trust in the physician may be more important than the biochemical effects of medication itself. Cardiac patients have been known to languish when their physicians become ill. Often there are several courses of treatment that could be tried, and the decision may not always rest with the physician, or even with the patient, but with the patient's family. On the other hand, too much knowledge is not always helpful either. Physicians do not treat themselves, nor should they treat their own family members. Fine physicians respect their own limits and fallibility.

Theology too is based on more than knowledge and sound judgment. While, as in medicine, there may be spontaneous spiritual transformations that point to the objective power of God to heal without our cooperation, most reform takes place more gradually and in a broader context. Usually

---

6. In medicine theoretical models are often modified by experimental trials. In theology, practice has often guided theory, following the ancient rule *lex orandi lex credendi*. A modern example of practice altering theory is the development of neoclassical theism to correct what from a Christian perspective was the difficulty with classical theism that God could not be involved with the world.

7. Another example would be the desire to enrich language for God beyond the monarchical and feudal language that once seemed definitive, but now is seen by many as inadequate to capture fully the grace and mercy of God.

the believer must trust God, be acquainted with the teachings of the church, participate in rites and practices of the church, be nourished by a supportive community, and be offered interpretations of the texts and traditions of the faith that fit the believer's circumstance. In short, trust and obedience are central to the successful practice of medicine and theology.[8]

Now, of course, theology, like medicine, contains elements of risk and uncertainty that can never be overcome. Even the hardest scientific core of medicine, medications, and diagnostic tests contains elements of uncertainty. Some patients will get better without intervention, while others will succumb to their illnesses regardless of care. A diagnostic screening tool, like the common Pap smear, may return up to 20 percent false negatives. On the theological side, some persons will succeed in resisting the grace of God even under the care of the best interpreters, while others will never mature spiritually no matter how gifted the rhetor; God's grace will transform others to their surprise and in spite of their efforts to avoid God. Good interpretation, like good medicine, is helpful but is neither foolproof nor essential.

At the same time, there is fine medical and theological practice, just as there is malpractice. Medical practices like bleeding and poultices proved to be harmful rather than salutary and so were abandoned. Similarly in theology, ascetic practices like starvation and deprivation of human contact were once thought to bring people to God but are now seen as detrimental to human flourishing. Theological and medical knowledge is revisable within limits set by their respective traditions. One strives constantly for excellent medical and theological practice, knowing that there will always be instances of malpractice by incompetent practitioners, along with improvements through continued research. Evidence of malpractice or greed in medicine is troubling but not a good reason to turn to shamanic practices instead. Theological malpractice should likewise stimulate a desire to encourage the highest integrity among its practitioners rather than a rush to dismantle or abandon the tradition.

Truth in both theology and medicine is malleable. It involves unknowns and risks, and calls for faith. But the analogy with medicine calls

---

8. The importance of trust and obedience in both medicine and theology does not, of course, deny that both arts may be used improperly and need to be examined critically or censured at times. But this model is developed not for corrupt but for healthy and proper instances of medical and theological practice.

for caution, because while some medications have unknown or poorly understood mechanisms, many are well understood and experimentally documented. There may be considerably greater uncertainty regarding the reality of God than there is about clinical pharmacology, although beliefs about God, like our understanding of health and disease, are refined through clinical practice. While medicine and theology contain elements of mystery, the mystery may be greater in theology, although the degree of trust necessary to garner the fruits of these arts may not be.

Yet broad similarities remain. Successful practice in either field requires skilled judgment of the facts, some of which, like the actions of lithium or other drugs undergoing testing, are gathered inductively; in a similar manner, knowledge of the power of God may legitimately be derived from the experiences of transformed believers.[9] In short, belief in the power of the Holy Spirit, prayer, the sacraments, and the doctrine of the atonement may strain credulity no more than faith in aspirin, which may fail to cure a simple headache.

The contemporary situation has brought into full view the subjective side of the medical and theological arts. While God's grace may be effective even in the most unsuspecting individual, it probably flourishes best, like medical treatment, under proper conditions. For the grace of God, those conditions include receptivity to God, trust in the rites of the church, and the support of a worshiping community. Like medical science, God of course sometimes works miracles, and he may be rebuffed.[10] And like all medications, in inexpert hands, the power of God for good may be distorted, as the history of the church well attests. Yet the proper practice of Christian interpretation, like the proper practice of medicine, serves as a source of healing and direction for honorable living.

Effective theological practice and effective medical practice depend, in short, upon the moral integrity and training of the practitioner, the engagement of the interpreter with the subject, and the element of trust between the parties involved. Yet neither discipline is ever free of mystery

9. See Patrick Sherry, *Spirit, Saints, and Immortality* (Albany: State Univ. of New York Press, 1984); and Grace Jantzen, "Conspicuous Sanctity and Religious Belief," in Abraham and Holtzer, eds., *Rationality of Religious Belief,* pp. 121-40.

10. See Alston's discussion for the conditions under which sanctity is achieved, in William P. Alston, "The Fulfillment of Promises as Evidence for Religious Belief," in *Faith in Theory and Practice: Essays on Justifying Religious Belief,* ed. Elizabeth S. Radcliffe and Carol J. White (Chicago: Open Court, 1993), pp. 1-34.

and risk. Theology should be as trusted and criticized as medicine and medicine should be as criticized and trusted as theology.

In this view of things, modern men and women may be comfortable enough with theological claims to trust a Christian worldview even if there are points at which they may disagree with that view. A cautious critical realism, like that at work in medical practice, is not the same thing as a naive realism that accepts all theological claims at face value. Instead, mature Christian belief can accept the need to adjust theological language and even doctrines and to admit the existence of failure in theology and the life of the church. Nor should the fact that the conditions for effective theological treatment are not always optimum discourage Christian belief. All of these difficulties also exist in modern medicine.

What does this argument for thinking of theologians as moral physicians have to do with the claim to truth made in the interpretation of texts? The point is that religious interpreters claim that their interpretations refer to the realities of God and of salvation. They make this claim not simply on the grounds of their being part of an interpretive community, but on the basis of their clinical success rate. That is, religious interpreters help people to lead morally and spiritually salutary lives. To make sound interpretive judgments, we need empirical evidence, in the form of transformed or deformed lives.

Religious interpreters are open to conversation, as Donald Marshall suggests. They remain open in order to specify and refine the claims they make as well as the manner in which those claims are applied. But there are limits to that openness, for religious interpreters must remain responsible to the foundational principles of their faith as they make practical recommendations for the cure of souls on a broad scale. This is to say that the formulation of rules is not only not "images of the world," as Marshall suggests, but those rules are also not only the "interpretations formed by the individual or taken over from the repertory stored up in his culture." The power of a coherent narrative to guide the good life does, in a broad sense, subordinate itself to general propositions about the goodness and sinfulness of human persons, the grace of God, the authority of Christ, and the hope of resurrection.

In conclusion, I wish to suggest, contra Marshall, that there are universal truths claimed by theology — notably its doctrines that provide standards for Christian interpretation just as medical research provides standards for clinical medicine. Both are necessary, but must be employed judiciously and with a degree of flexibility adapted to the circumstance and need. In this way, interpretation, while it does not free itself from the contingencies of time and space, makes what might be called soft epistemic claims. There is more at work in Christian interpretation than conceptual clarity. There is also the bedrock of Christian doctrine to which interpretation is called back and that proves as effective in its sphere as medicine is in its sphere. Interpretation requires both *techne* and *phronesis,* technology and wisdom. And which among the scientific disciplines will give up discerning judgment, theoretical revision in the face of clinical experience, trust in the bedrock principles of the discipline, and adaptation in the face of circumstance?

From Suspicion to Retrieval:
Hermeneutics and the Human Sciences

Sliding in All Directions?
Social Hermeneutics from
Suspicion to Retrieval

DAVID LYON

For many, it seems, the postmodern is a threat of some magnitude. Not only religion, but even good old science is questioned as a reliable way of finding out about the world. "Knowledge," we are told, must abandon its singular claims and give away to "knowledges." One's subjective stance is all that counts any more.

It seems that anyone can claim that their identity — and thus their right to voice a viewpoint or their right to special treatment — is to be found in their peculiar ethnic or social situation. Thus, as they say, "anything goes."

Leonard Cohen captures this sense of a slippery, fissiparous, evaporating world in "The Future":

> Things are going to slide, slide in all directions
> Won't be nothing you can measure any more
>
> . . . a breaking of the ancient Western code
> your private life will suddenly explode.

The first step is to say that our attempts to understand anything will reflect our peculiar historical horizon. The next is to conclude that there is nothing beyond those horizons; nothing we share in common that might transcend our historical, cultural niche. Everything is relative, so we can be sure of nothing.

The postmodern, according to its critics, is associated with relativism as a kind of yeast that has infected the whole batch of dough.[1] One discipline that could be charged with warming the dough so that the yeast would do its work is sociology. Sociology softens certainty by pointing to other cultures, other times, where things are thought or done differently. Surely different cannot be wrong? So the argument goes, sometimes *ad absurdum*.

A sort of selective amnesia is evident here, and a recovery of memory may help to throw fresh light on the postmodern condition. Starting with sociology, let us inquire into the source of one of its modes of interpretation. We do not have to travel back too far to find that sociological hermeneutics began life, ironically, as an extension of biblical hermeneutics.

What happened in biblical hermeneutics? What began as a science of interpretation, for better understanding the text, has often ended as a pretext for doubting or even discarding the text. What the Reformers intended as the effect of their interpretive studies — to bring better understanding of biblical texts and submission to them — has sometimes been diluted through hermeneutic developments. And in contributing to a swing toward private interpretation, the Reformation tradition has often helped to blunt the power of the biblical texts to provide a critique of the self and of society.

In one sense, postmodernism stands at the end of the Reformation tradition's interpretive practices. In addition to being an intellectual movement, postmodernism is also a social phenomenon that has brought hermeneutic questions down to earth, to the daily routine. That is why it affects all of us, and why Leonard Cohen sings about it over the radio. It is also why we cannot any longer neatly split the epistemological from the ethical.[2]

The debate over hermeneutics in the postmodern world, paradoxically, may offer us a chance to resist relativism. Indeed, if the postmodern debate leads to a recovery of memory, this may provide for a recovery of the social for sociology and even of the Bible for Christianity. Still more scandalously, the postmodern experience opens doors for dialogue, so that the biblical text may enter into a conversation with social reality and social reality with the biblical text.[3]

1. See, e.g., the attack of Ernest Gellner in his *Postmodernism, Reason and Religion* (New York: Routledge, 1992).

2. Gianni Vattimo, e.g., makes this point in *The Transparent Society,* trans. David Webb (Baltimore: Johns Hopkins Univ. Press, 1992).

3. Perhaps the reason why the emphasis is on the social is itself postmodern. After modernity has struggled for two centuries to reconcile liberty and equality, the unsolved problem of fraternity comes to the fore.

Sociological Hermeneutics

Sociological hermeneutics grew out of biblical hermeneutics and may be traced to the work of Wilhelm Dilthey, the son of a Protestant pastor. Dilthey's central concern was the philosophical foundations of the human sciences. The life-experience of the interpreter provides the crucial point of contact with the text, Dilthey believed. He distanced himself from those who believed that the human "sciences" could be built on the model of physics. In this view, both the author and interpreter are positioned on the horizon of their historical moment.

For Dilthey, the nearest thing to a transcendental principle that might go beyond the historical moment is *Erlebnis,* or lived experience. This lived experience sets humans apart from nature and requires that a different kind of "science" than physics be practiced to understand human experience and texts. Causal explanation may play a part in social science, but only when combined with the art of understanding, or *Verstehen.* "The relation of one mind to another which we call understanding is a basic fact of human life," argued Georg Simmel, one of Dilthey's contemporaries.

A number of sociologists, to be sure, did their best to make causal explanation the centerpiece of the sociological discipline. Émile Durkheim and Max Weber, for example, differ from Simmel in denigrating lay knowledge. For them, sociology is superior to common experience. The rationality of actors is always suspect and subject to correction by sociology.

Zygmunt Bauman blames Kant for this situation. Kant's philosopher is no mere artist occupying "himself with conceptions, but a lawgiver legislating for human reason."[4] Along with Descartes and Locke, Kant would help impose the model of foundational philosophy on two centuries of thought. But as Bauman also observes, foundational philosophy as legislative reason finds its correlate in the foundational politics of the rising modern state. In sociology, Kant's legacy could be seen both in the assumption of the false consciousness of ordinary people in everyday life *and* in the promise of the rational organization of the human condition.

Interpretive sociology of the kind promoted by Dilthey, however, did not just disappear. By the 1960s, sociology's legislative reason was coming

4. Zygmunt Bauman, *Intimations of Postmodernity* (New York: Routledge, 1992), p. 116.

under attack both for its reductionism and its conservatism. Talcott Parsons's scheme, for example, was taken to be a justification of the American way of life and its imperialism. The attack upon rationalistic reductionism in sociology coincided with the discovery of the relevance of phenomenology for the discipline. Erving Goffman and Harold Garfinkel in particular returned to the world of everyday life and to the actors' "definition of the situation."

The insights of Goffman, Garfinkel, and others have now been integrated into the more general hermeneutic turn in the social sciences. Much social analysis now recognizes that mutual understanding, as Hans-Georg Gadamer argued, is the means of sustaining the routines of everyday life and that thus "interpretation is not only a specialized method of social science but a particular accomplishment that makes social life possible."[5] Researchers must in some way share in the life-world of the people studied in order to interpret it, while also recognizing that their interpretations enter into the fabric of the social life being studied.

The changes that took place in sociological theory several decades ago were accompanied by a new sensitivity to groups long subordinated by capitalism, industrialism, colonialism, and patriarchy. Until then, the main opposition to the logic of modernity had come from labor movements, but during and after the 1960s there was a more general rising awareness of the negative backlash of modernity.

As labor movements themselves fell on hard times, a whole range of movements appeared in their place: green, feminist, ethnic, nationalist, and, later, gay and lesbian. As they became stronger and more self-confident, such groups questioned not only the social arrangements that had limited them for so long, but also the ideologies that had justified such silencing.

The prime example of this was feminist theory, which begins by criticizing dominant ways of doing sociology. Dorothy Smith, for instance, argues that until recently, women's experience was systematically excluded from the patriarchal "relations of ruling" within the sociological profession. Her critique of objectified subjects leads her to say that sociology must get to know the directly experienced world from within. "The presence, concerns and experience of the sociologist as knower and discoverer"

---

5. Steven Seidman, in *Culture and Society: Contemporary Debates,* ed. Jeffrey C. Alexander and Steven Seidman (New York: Cambridge Univ. Press, 1990), p. 217.

must appear within sociology. From this standpoint, the sociologist can open up and explore "the objectified relations of ruling as what people actually do."[6]

Long suppressed by legislative reason, the interpretive reason championed by Dilthey resurfaced. But it is important to note what kind of interpretive reason became central. As Bauman notes, Schleiermacher's and Dilthey's hermeneutic aims had remained those of correcting misunderstandings.

Toward the end of his life, however, Dilthey seemed to doubt the potential for historically privileged interpretation. It was left to Gadamer to spell out the implications of Dilthey's doubt. First, Gadamer concluded, the discovery of the true meaning of a text or a work of art is never finished, but is in fact an infinite process. From this it follows that professional hermeneutics is denied a special privilege. If we understand at all, Gadamer argued, it is enough to say that we understand in a different way. The very idea of privileged knowledge becomes nonsensical, and the plurality of interpretations is taken for granted. *Becoming* is everything.

Within the contingent world of contemporary theory, says Bauman, an obsessive search for community grows, what Michel Maffesoli calls "neo-tribalism."[7] Only tribal truths and tribal decisions about right and wrong can be made. One can enter or leave the tribe easily by means of self-identification. Thus, inquiry into the bases of knowledge or of ethics turns out to be sociological inquiry, given their social determination. And in such a world, says Bauman, sociology in general may "openly become what it was destined to be all along: the informed, systematic commentary on the knowledge of everyday life, a commentary that expands that knowledge while being fed into it and itself transformed in the process."[8]

This view of how sociology operates fits well with Anthony Giddens's view of the sociological task. It also connects with the structural conditions within which social analysis and theorizing are done.[9] In premodern societies tradition serves to integrate the reflexive monitoring of action with

6. Dorothy Smith, *The Conceptual Practices of Power: A Feminist Sociology of Knowledge* (Boston: Northeastern Univ. Press, 1990), pp. 22, 28.

7. Bauman, *Intimations of Postmodernity,* p. 136.

8. Bauman, *Intimations of Postmodernity,* p. 144.

9. What follows summarizes material found in Anthony Giddens, *The Consequences of Modernity* (Stanford: Stanford Univ. Press, 1990), pp. 36ff.

community organization. Reflexivity reinterprets and clarifies the tradition. The past, much more than the future, is the focus.

Reflexivity takes on a different character in modernity. In the contemporary world, it enters the processes that assure the reproduction of the system. The past is only important if it coincides with knowledge of the future. Tradition can still be justified, but it lacks authenticity, since it receives its identity only from the reflexivity of the modern. This modern reflexivity means that social practices are constantly examined in the light of new knowledge, which fundamentally alters their character.

It is not merely that we have to "know how to go on" (in Wittgenstein's sense). In modernity, avers Giddens, the "revision of convention" is "radicalized to apply (in principle) to all aspects of human life, including technological intervention into the material world."[10] If everything, including reflection, is reflected upon, even reason is subverted.

This process is intensified in the social sciences as their discourse reenters the very contexts it is analyzing. Despite the powerful appearance of scientific knowledge at the heart of the technological changes of modernity, the social sciences are implicated as much as technology in modern life, "since the chronic revision of social practices in the light of knowledge about those practices is part of that very tissue of modern institutions."[11] Markets and investment in economics, as well as the nuclear family and racial prejudice in sociology, both constitute social practices and serve as instruments for the interpretation of those practices.

Sociology thus plays a role within the reflexivity of modernity. Whether through the use of official or popular knowledge of ethnic, sexual, or work relations, sociology helps to constitute what we know as the modern world. From stabilizing or controlling social situations, this sociological intervention helps perpetuate the very alterations that it has set out to study.

Sliding in All Directions? Postmodern Hermeneutics

To many, the relativism and reflexivity of modernity makes it seem, as Leonard Cohen sings, that things are sliding in all directions. Whether in politics, art, or city planning, nothing seems certain any more. For many

10. Giddens, *Consequences of Modernity*, p. 49.
11. Giddens, *Consequences of Modernity*, p. 40.

Christian people, liberties taken with Scripture in the name of scholarship seem to mock the historic creeds of the church. Perhaps, they think, Schleiermacher started us down a slippery slope. Slithering helplessly down it, there is nothing to hold onto any more. Maybe religion's reality is social, after all, and the best bet is to adopt a sociological stance and be done with worry about the truth.

But to abandon belief in favor of social science seems not much better. Jean Baudrillard tells us there is no place for sociology any more because we have reached the "end of the social." If indeed the social ever existed at all, it has now dissolved in the force field between the masses and the media.[12] Opinion polls, statistical surveys, and audience ratings are all that is left of what was once thought to be the social. As Barry Smart observes, however, Baudrillard still uses the term *society,* even though much more could be said for doubting the usefulness of this term.[13]

The postmodern is often portrayed as being about endings (". . . it ain't going any further," sings Cohen) — not only the end of the author, but the end of the social, the end of history, and, of course, the end of modernity. What this last ending would mean is disputed and unclear. Even if in some circles the Enlightenment project is dismissed, its legacy lives on in democratic, organizational, and scientific practices. It may take different forms in Africa or on the Pacific Rim, but modernization is still evident there, too.

It is much more productive to conceive of the postmodern as a new way of approaching modernity, one that accepts the contradictions and ambiguities of modernity as "facts of life."[14] To do so is to avoid the temptation to periodize, as if the "end of modernity" could be dated — architecturally, 1973, politically, 1989, and so on. It also means that those adopting the different terminology of "late," "radicalized," "high," or "re-flexive" modernity can be seen as debating the same sets of issues with different emphases. As Barry Smart suggests, postmodernity "suggests not the passing of modernity, not the end of history or politics, not a nostalgic revival of a valued past, but a different way of relating to modern condi-

12. Jean Baudrillard, *In the Shadow of the Silent Majorities,* trans. Paul Foss, Paul Patton, and John Johnston (New York: Semiotext[e], 1983).

13. Barry Smart, *Postmodernity* (New York: Routledge, 1993), p. 56.

14. See the discussion of the meaning of the concept of postmodernity in David Lyon, *Postmodernity* (Minneapolis: Univ. of Minnesota Press, 1994).

tions and their consequences."[15] Postmodernity is in this sense a hermeneutic concept, a prism through which modernity is refracted in fresh
ways.[16]

Yet postmodern hermeneutics is different from the modern. Scien-
tism predominated within interpretive debates for well over a century, but
increasingly the idea has been questioned that truth can be reduced to
propositions confirmed by mathematical formulae. This means that hermeneutics comes to be seen as "practical philosophy" (especially following
Gadamer) and that it is also oriented toward ethics.

There are two striking facts about postmodern hermeneutics. One is
that for all their apparently relativistic tendencies, several postmodern com-
mentators strenuously deny that relativism is what they promote. The other
is that it is ethical rather than cognitive relativism that these same com-
mentators wish to deny most strenuously.

Postmodern societies produce surpluses. Two of the most important are
heresy production and risk production. That the two are closely related can be
shown in the work of the sociologist Peter Berger and Jean Baudrillard. Berger
has analyzed extensively the concept of the "heretical imperative" operating in
postmodern societies. According to Berger, that imperative is one of the great
relativizing forces of contemporary life and lies behind the ever-increasing
emphasis upon tolerance in postmodern culture. And just as the heretical
imperative has driven people to sharp conflicts of values and beliefs, the
coming of the "risk society" has left those who live in postmodern societies
with agonizing existential difficulties in their daily lives and few means of
confronting or coping with those difficulties. The work of Baudrillard provides
valuable resources for understanding the limits of tolerance through the
concept of those social limits needed to combat the negative effects of risk.[17]

Barry Smart picks up Berger's concept of the heretical imperative,
noting that in modern societies, where "heresy" sounds out of place, one
can still observe public demonstrations against films like "The Last Temptation of Christ" or view the public burning of books like The Satanic Verses.
Tradition here confronts modernity, showing, as Berger says, worldview

15. Smart, Postmodernity, pp. 151-52.
16. Lyon, Postmodernity, chap. 6.
17. See the critique by Sander Griffioen and Richard Mouw, Pluralisms and
Horizons: An Essay in Christian Public Philosophy (Grand Rapids: Eerdmans, 1993), pp.
53-54.

competition and a "crisis of belief."[18] For him, modernity is a "great relativizing cauldron." But Smart cautions that in addition to modern doubt
and postmodern transgression, ancient belief is also present here.

The growing power of social actors is often seen as characteristic of
reflective modernization. Berger, for instance, is certainly right to stress the
context of increased choice today.[19] But this increase in choices may signal not
so much the rejection of all rules as the quest for new ones. Smart even ponders
"the possibility of a reconstituted modernity. Calling modernity to account,
demanding that costs as well as benefits are acknowledged, the unintended
consequences and limits recognized, postmodernity re-presents modernity."[20]

The fact that in the academy one can no longer assume the superiority
or reliability of the Western way of science, that in politics and industry
one can no longer assume that new technologies have generally benign
effects, or that in the church it is less and less usual to find expressions of
Constantinian approaches does not mean that relativism rules. Indeed,
Emilio Betti, for whom hermeneutics was vital to social well-being, observed that the recognition that all interpretation is open to correction
should promote greater tolerance without abandoning the search for truth.
In an ever more postmodern vein, Gianni Vattimo sees as emancipatory
the hermeneutic turn away from the stable, fixed, and permanent.[21]

It is one thing to shed the shackles of legislative reason and politics,
another to find new ways forward. What is the basis of critique when science
can no longer legitimate itself and when the notion of an epistemological
guarantee is itself suspect?[22] When heresy has become the universal condition, appropriate "ways forward" are bound to be contentious and in-

18. Peter Berger, *The Heretical Imperative: Contemporary Possibilities of Religious
Affirmation* (Garden City, N.Y.: Anchor Press, 1979), p. 18.

19. The matter of "more choice" is, of course, contested terrain. One might argue
that while the old structuring based on material production has diminished in power,
newer structuring, based on cultural production — a "mode of information" — may
be emerging as new communication and information technologies proliferate. See, *inter
alia*, Mark Poster, *The Second Media Age* (Cambridge: Polity Press, 1995); and David
Lyon, *The Electronic Eye: The Rise of Surveillance Society* (Minneapolis: Univ. of Minnesota Press, 1994).

20. Smart, *Postmodernity*, p. 116.

21. Vattimo, *Transparent Society*.

22. Jean-François Lyotard, *The Postmodern Condition: A Report on Knowledge*,
trans. Geoff Bennington and Brian Massumi (Minneapolis: Univ. of Minnesota Press,
1984), p. 40.

complete, and many postmodern writers emphasize that this is what it means to live *in* postmodernity. "Living amidst such a world of difference," says Smart, "it is necessary to nurture the conditions conducive to a tolerant and pluralistic social order."[23]

Much turns, then, on tolerance as a virtue. But even this requires further definition and clarity. Does tolerance, for instance, mean accepting the equality of all truth claims? Does tolerance mean indifference to or acquiescence in injustice or suffering?[24] In order to get a handle on these issues it is worth examining them in the light of the other current surplus, risk.

Ulrich Beck's work on the "risk society" has established itself as a contemporary sociological classic.[25] Beck's work helps to refocus sociology after the demise of grand theories like Marxism or functionalism. He argues that modern societies produce not only a wealth surplus, but also a risk surplus. Risk avoidance and risk management have now become two of the twentieth century's most pressing problems.

Modernity alters its character with this shift, according to Beck. Science and technology produce both the problems and the suggested solutions. Indeed, science is needed to perceive the problem at all. Then science gives the illusion of control over destiny; risks are "calculable." This in turn connects with a point already made about reflexivity: the future is colonized through risk assessment. In this account, science is a kind of double agent, serving both the cause of technology and those who would put a check on the advance and abuse of technology. Meanwhile, risks escalate, extending in time and space. Ozone layer leaks, for example, are intergenerational and global in scope.

Modernity, in this view, looks to some like a juggernaut, largely out of control, scarcely steerable.[26] We have all become aware of high consequence risks confronting us, such as global overconsumption. These risks are both remote and simultaneously experienced as personal risk. None of

23. Smart, *Postmodernity,* p. 126.

24. Such questions are addressed helpfully in Griffioen and Mouw, *Pluralisms and Horizons.*

25. Ulrich Beck, *Risk Society: Towards a New Modernity,* trans. Mark Ritter (Newbury Park, Calif.: Sage, 1992).

26. Giddens, *Consequences of Modernity;* see also Langdon Winner, *Autonomous Technology: Technics-out-of-Control as a Theme in Political Thought* (Cambridge, Mass.: MIT Press, 1977).

us can avoid them, and we too calculate what we do in relation to each risk. To drive on the highway, to take a plane, even to switch on a light to eat a fast-food burger is to take a risk. Choice impinges constantly.

On a day-to-day existential level we all face risks, which means that the large processes of a global nature intersect routinely with daily lives. In detraditionalized contexts, the self now has to cope with these without the benefit of traditional certainties. Negotiating lifestyle choices out of a range of options is part of what it is to construct self-identity at the end of the twentieth century, and thus includes risk calculation.[27] But it can be a lonely and agonizing task, given that we are forced back onto our own resources by the lack of help from either tradition (discounted) or science (demor-alized).

The other side of the coin is that the same postmodern societies are by definition consumer societies. Risk production accelerates with rising demand for consumer goods to satiate constantly stimulated desires. Most calculation is thus economic calculation, geared to self-gratification, and galvanized not only by advertising companies but by governments that treat citizens as consumers and encourage them to perceive their personal aspira-tions as "human rights."

So while modernity-generated risks proliferate, they impinge on the daily lives of people who are forced to choose between the demoralized discourse of efficiency or the consumer discourse of individual hedonism as the means of making sense of these global-personal extremities. But is Beck entirely correct? Have we really been atomized, individuated, isolated in this way? Or is there still a "social realm?"

A Hermeneutics of Retrieval

Until now, much of what has passed as postmodern hermeneutics has been in the vein of "the hermeneutics of suspicion."[28] The ghost of Nietzsche hovers not far in the background of contemporary theories of interpreta-

---

27. Anthony Giddens, *Modernity and Self-Identity: Self and Society in the Late Modern Age* (Stanford: Stanford Univ. Press, 1991).

28. The phrase originated with Paul Ricoeur. See Paul Ricoeur, *Freud and Philos-ophy: An Essay on Interpretation,* trans. Denis Savage (New Haven: Yale Univ. Press, 1970), p. 30.

tion, haunting Heidegger, Derrida, and Foucault. We find power in knowledge, whether patriarchal, technocratic, capitalist, or whatever, and like tracker dogs we can sniff it out of the most unlikely places. With not only a deceased deity, but the demise of erstwhile demi-gods, including Marx or Freud, all is permitted. Anything goes.

The necessary task performed or assisted by the hermeneutics of suspicion includes the dethroning of Western rationality, the debunking of democratic progress through social engineering, the dismantling of male privilege, and the decolonization of the Third World.[29] Whether in the academy, church, industry, or media, we are becoming increasingly aware of the need to question the status quo of hierarchy and convention, to see whether we are silencing others and preventing their full participation in social life.

What is missing is a sense of just what might make up that "social life." Impatience with the silliness of "political correctness" is symptomatic of a more general concern that, having deconstructed *ad infinitum,* we are still left with great uncertainty about how to go on. This uncertainty is made the more poignant and pressing by the accumulation of risks. Jesus, seen by some as the paradigmatic master of suspicion in his deconstructing of self-serving Pharisaic Jewish law, never rested with suspicion but sought to retrieve. "You have heard it said . . ." is suspicion. "But I say unto you . . ." is retrieval.[30]

As it happens, complacent satisfaction with the mere hermeneutics of suspicion seems to be more characteristic of trendy postmodern theorists than it does of some mainstream postmodern authors. In several of this latter group, including Derrida, Lyotard, Paul Virilio, and Luce Irigaray, there is an ethical impulse that questions moral absolutism but also seeks to find some alternative to it. Some continue to toy with the possibility of aesthetic approaches, while others, significantly, draw upon the work of Emmanuel Levinas.[31]

---

29. Merold Westphal, *Suspicion and Faith: The Religious Uses of Modern Atheism* (Grand Rapids: Eerdmans, 1993).

30. Ulrich Beck, Anthony Giddens, and Scott Lash, *Reflexive Modernization: Politics, Tradition, and Aesthetics in the Modern Social Order* (Cambridge: Polity Press, 1994), p. 146. I want to use this term in a way that is informed by Christian commitments and thus may well be unacceptable to Lash.

31. Martin Jay, "Is There a Poststructuralist Ethics?" in *Force Fields: Between Intellectual History and Cultural Critique* (New York: Routledge, 1993), pp. 38-48.

Scott Lash proposes a "hermeneutics of retrieval" that "will not unendingly sweep away foundations but will attempt to lay open the ontological foundations of communal being-in-the-world." It will not "chronically defer and deny meaning" and will "instead of marveling at the free play of the signifier, modestly 'look beneath' that signifier to gain access to the shared meanings which are the conditions of existence, indeed *are* the very existence, of the 'we.'"[32]

Lash draws on Dick Hebdige and Jürgen Habermas. He respects but finally rejects Giddens as too individualistic and Charles Taylor as too Christian but follows Bourdieu for his emphasis on the "habitus," where "truth is neither conceptual nor mimetic, but becomes evident through shared practices."[33] Unhappy with much sociological communitarianism that assumes away power and conservatively presumes consensus, he finds in Pierre Bourdieu a plausible emphasis on power struggles over forms of life. Today, thinks Lash, these struggles take place in the "mode of information." Here too are new opportunities for the "we," new cultural communities in the structure of information and communication.[34]

Searching for a "notion of involvement in communal practices out of which self grows," Lash finds clues in Seyla Benhabib's stress on "care."[35] Having linked it with Foucault's later subjectivist turn and with Heidegger's "concern" for things and for others, however, Lash leaves the question of care hanging. But care deserves to be explored further. While it is not certain that Foucault really came around to "care" in the end, it is certainly the case that he missed it in his best-known work.

In *Discipline and Punish*, for instance, where he builds on the pivotal significance of the Panopticon prison architecture, Foucault simply follows Jeremy Bentham's attempt to create a mechanical, automatic means of social control. He shows how power is maintained by a system of unseen observers whose invisible work teaches us to seek out self-serving power strategies wherever we find them. Analysis of electronic surveillance finds just such power flows in contemporary social control.

32. Lash in Beck, Giddens, and Lash, *Reflexive Modernization*, p. 157.
33. Lash in Beck, Giddens, and Lash, *Reflexive Modernization*, p. 157.
34. This is a line of analysis worth pursuing. The problem is how the increased stretching of social relations in space and time can actually be characterized by the "care" for which Lash and Benhabib would also argue.
35. Selya Benhabib, *Situating the Self: Gender, Community, and Postmodernism in Contemporary Ethics* (New York: Routledge, 1992).

But if Foucault had taken his own genealogical approach further, he might have found a different account of the situation. For Bentham was a self-conscious secular social reformer who wanted his rational schemes entirely to supplant previous "theological" conceptions. The omniscience of the Panopticon is deliberately secular, but he makes a fatal error in quoting from Psalm 139 in his epigram to the Panopticon plan. Even a cursory reading of the psalm reveals another narrative. In the name of rational certainty Bentham tried to abolish ambiguity, but the psalm has no such assurance.

In Psalm 139 omniscience is indeed a means of moral suasion, of stimulating self-discipline ("see if there is any offensive way in me") but also of gentle love ("even there your hand will guide me, your right hand will hold me fast"). Power control is only part of the story; the other part is patience and care. In this account we find not a mere discourse of cynical power, but a source of critical distance, a means of critique that might not only question limitless coercion but also indicate the constructive contribution of care in surveillance systems.[36]

Bauman has taken up the issue of care in what might be called his sociological hermeneutic of the "other." For Bauman, postmodernity pushes us to "moral responsibility as the first reality of the self," which means "being *for* the Other before one can be with the Other." Here is no foundation for morality but an a priori moral self that precedes the social self (which is the reverse of what modernity taught).

Bauman obtains much leverage from Levinas, for whom the subject is — like the Samaritan in the Gospels — laid claim to by the "other."[37] Levinas, a post-Holocaust Jew, finds in the face of the other an echo of the words "thou shall not kill," thus connecting commitment to others with the commands of God. He sees the significance of the other emblematically in the widow, the orphan, the stranger, the helpless or marginalized; in other words, on anyone who has valid claims on us.[38]

And so a different kind of hermeneutic circle appears to open up. This retrieval involves remembering the care spoken of in the Jewish and

---

36. David Lyon, "Bentham's Panopticon: From Moral Architecture to Electronic Surveillance," *Queen's Quarterly* 98 (Fall 1991); Lyon, *Electronic Eye*.

37. Zygmunt Bauman, *Postmodern Ethics* (Oxford: Blackwell, 1993).

38. See John Caputo, "The Good News About Alterity: Derrida and Theology," *Faith and Philosophy* 10, no. 4 (1993).

Christian Scriptures, connecting it with the ontological situation of communal being-in-the-world, and using this hermeneutic to interpret contemporary social situations and processes. Of course, this exploration could be pursued — to examine the social implications of the Trinity, in the *imago dei*, and in other ways as well — but this assumes that we can also retrieve the text containing these ideas.

But if only half of the story is told with regard to the self, leaving us with a bankrupt, individualized self rather than a communal one, then perhaps only half of the story is also present in some versions of the "risk society" thesis. In the hands of some postmoderns, the risks we confront add up to a kind of permanent apocalypse, seen in films such as "Blade Runner" or in books such as *Panic Encyclopedia*. As Martin Jay observes, the apocalyptic genre used to have two sides, both destructive judgment and revelation or disclosure.[39] The secularization of providence into progress and then into nihilism has in the past two centuries shriveled hope, leaving only vestiges and residues in place of the fully-orbed apocalyptic.

What has happened to providentialism is a story in itself, but it is worth asking if components of the Jewish and Christian narratives of creation and providence really have nothing to say to the postmodern dilemmas and ambiguities of person and planet. The problem of suffering, which has a high profile in Bauman's work and thus reveals him as a critical theorist, finds classic Christian understanding in the cross of Christ.[40] That this has been eclipsed does not mean that its power to act as a hermeneutic key is somehow vitiated. In biblical terms both the suffering of human victims and the suffering of the earth are understood in relation to the cross. On the other side of the cross, however, tears are wiped away *and* the groaning creation finds its destiny in the new heavens and earth.

Sliding helplessly over those slippery postmodern surfaces is not our only option. Contemporary Christians could do far worse than to contribute to the hermeneutics of retrieval by reintroducing central themes of the biblical narrative into current debates in social theory.[41] They could do so not by way of a new narrative handed down from above, or even as a

---

39. Jay, *Force Fields.*
40. Zygmunt Bauman, *Modernity and the Holocaust* (Ithaca, N.Y.: Cornell Univ. Press, 1989).
41. John Milbank, in his *Theology and Social Theory: Beyond Secular Reason* (Oxford: Blackwell, 1990).

guaranteed simple solution to complex human struggles, but as an offer of a different perspective, making witness within the maelstrom of post-modern debate. Is it only my imagination, or does the gospel not resonate with just those issues that make our world "postmodern"?

Coda

In the light of the paradoxes and ambiguities of hermeneutic development, what can be done? How am I, as a confessing Christian, to do my work in sociology today? Clearly, some still think the sociological calling and Christianity incompatible. I find these challenging and exciting times, not least because just those themes that are central to my commitments seem to speak relevantly to the deepest issues raised by the analysis of the post-modern. As I consider, for example, my work on the social aspects of communication and information technologies, these are some lessons of the preceding survey.

First, recognize reflexivity. I have to be aware of my own complicity in the social institutions I attempt to analyze. Concepts get woven back into those situations — think of the Internet and Marshall McLuhan's "global village!" — helping to (re)constitute them. I am not uninvolved, detached, even though I may use techniques that give me some distance from, or means of comparison with, the object of study.

Second, abandon legislation. The idea of imposing interpretations on social actors whose understanding of social situations is supposedly inferior to mine seems quite unacceptable. Legislative reason is imperial, authoritarian, paternalistic, patriarchal. To interpret, from an acknowledged perspective, may be seen as bearing witness. This is the sociologist as servant of society, not as powerful social engineer.

Third, focus on otherness. It is easy to speak from a specific ethnic, cultural, gender, political, or religious position, and reflexivity is a reminder of this. It is far harder to step into the shoes of the other, the more so because of popular postmodern denial that this is possible.[42] Otherness (alterity) focuses on the claims laid on us by others (not on our own claims to "rights"). These issues gain new immediacy in discussions of virtual

42. This is a controversy well beyond the confines of sociology alone, of course. See, e.g., Edward Said, *Orientalism* (New York: Pantheon, 1978).

communities of cyberspace. What are the emerging social conventions of the Internet, and how can otherness and care be expressed within computer-mediated relations?

Fourth, seek purpose. Teleology has suffered some nasty shocks under the impact of modernization. Hope vested in broader purposes beyond the humanly generated has shrunk not only mere temporal horizons but has been unmasked (suspicion!) as, for instance, an ephemeral concern with "newness." But the postmodern offers the opportunity not only to deny purpose but also to affirm it in new — or revived — neoprovidential ways.

So, sliding in all directions? Yes, Leonard Cohen rightly discerns a sense of slippery postmodern surfaces that are so disorienting, so unsafe. My effort to recover a perspective on what has happened between biblical, sociological, and postmodern hermeneutics is not intended to render the world of interpretation any safer by offering some supposed *terra firma* rather than the ice. But neither do I think we are condemned forever to slide in all directions.

A hermeneutics of retrieval can operate alongside of the hermeneutics of suspicion, allowing us, through dialogue with some postmodern writers, to speak to real concerns of people in their daily lives, now irrevocably bound up with global conditions. That this effort may be scorned, spurned, or just sidelined as one view among many is a palpable risk. But the bigger risk is that a Christian perspective within the debate would disappear by default. There is no risk-free space.

Baptizing a Social Reading: Theology, Hermeneutics, and Postmodernity

WILLIE JAMES JENNINGS

With that, he hid himself; and pondering
the speech that seemed to me so menacing,
I turned my steps to meet the ancient poet.

Dante, *The Divine Comedy: Inferno*[1]

[Sociology] . . . may "come out" — openly become what it was destined to be all along: the informed, systematic commentary on the knowledge of daily life, a commentary that expands that knowledge while being fed into it and itself transformed in the process.

Zygmunt Bauman, *Intimations of Postmodernity*[2]

David Lyon has presented a courageous call to the sociological guild and has discerned a moment of possibility for Christians within the postmodern condition, this time of flood in which all things have come

---

1. Dante, *The Divine Comedy: Inferno,* trans. Allen Mandelbaum (Berkeley: Univ. of California Press, 1980), 10:121-23.
2. Zygmunt Bauman, *Intimations of Postmodernity* (London: Routledge, 1992), p. 144.

loose. The only proper conclusion to his discernment is to allow a complete transformation of sociology: sociology must be reinvented as a theological and ethical discourse upon the social. We of course should press for a *Christian* theological discourse upon the social. This would allow us to move beyond the hermeneutics of suspicion, which yet remains beneath much of postmodern thought and ethics.

Lyon suggests that if one takes postmodernity seriously as an unsafe but creative theoretical space, this opens the way to reconsidering the categories of both hermeneutics and history as they relate to sociological vision. What if history as told and conceived by Christians could be retrieved as a *living* fiction of the social, and hermeneutics be retrieved as the formation of social *illusion* that does not lie? This way of viewing history and hermeneutics is intended to face the existing intersection between information hyper-dissemination, cultural production and reproduction, and aggressive consumerism that are, in fact, only attuned to illusion. Standing at this intersection, modern Western people only hear a word of truth as an agreed-upon deception, a *policed* relativism. Thus sociology, as a discipline that seeks to discern the truth of human sociality and its constitutive conditions, faces a moment of truth. Can it deliver on the historic promise of its discipline: objective vision (i.e., truth) of the social, without being destroyed by the hermeneutics of suspicion or dismissed by a policing relativism?[3]

At this moment in history, theology (and by implication the church) must reassert truth without seeking its reestablishment. For many, this is a very frightening prospect, but these fears are for the most part misplaced. Christian truth understood as a powerful assertion aimed at popular Western culture would help to overcome the theological anemia that affects many of our churches and educational institutions. This anemia is in great measure produced by the exhausting effort of *Christians* seeking to maintain a culturally based vision of unified truth that in effect does not need Christianity for its own integrity.[4] In fact such a vision of truth has often

3. See Anthony Giddens and Jonathan H. Turner, eds. *Social Theory Today* (California: Stanford Univ. Press, 1987), pp. 1-10.

4. See Stanley Hauerwas, *Dispatches from the Front: Theological Engagements with the Secular* (Durham, N.C.: Duke Univ. Press, 1994), pp. 5-28, 91-106; and Stanley Hauerwas et al., *Theology Without Foundations: Religious Practice and the Future of Theological Truth* (Nashville: Abingdon Press, 1994).

found Christian faith to be a hindrance to the establishing of truth; it sees faith as the promotion of illusion and fiction. Rather than contend with such a critique or support the process of reestablishment (which only gives life to new forms of critique), I propose a *truthful way* of seeing reality that can make use of the dynamic located in notions like illusion and fiction while not being captured by such notions.

This "illusion" of which we Christians speak gives us a way of seeing that is nothing less than sight to the blind. This "fiction" to which we testify also gives strength to the weak through the power to challenge and to exorcise evil from a society that is not yet what it will be in God. Lyon is right to invoke an eschatological vision, which is the original scandal of the message of Jesus, that the kingdom has come in this one man and the world is forever changed. To press this needed baptism of sociology and to resurrect theology as a "scandalous eschatological discourse," however, we must augment Lyon's vital and provocative narrative by acknowledging the place of reading in grasping the social text, the place of knowledge in recognizing what is to be read, and the place of a hermeneutics of retrieval in the larger scheme of things.

The Place of Reading: Reading as Writing, Writing as Praying (or) Playing

David Lyon notes that the current debates over hermeneutics paradoxically offer a way forward beyond relativism. This is the case, ironically enough, because the theoretical and existential "suspicion" that drives postmodern critique has itself finally come under critique. This "suspicion," which has always mirrored the growing sense of risk that permeates our postindustrial societies, now itself demands a kind of management. Hermeneutic explorers in our moment in history are now in search of an anti-foundationalist, anti-essentialist mode *of suspicion*, wanting neither the desert island of past foundations nor the continuation of the unending chaos of the open high seas of foundationless foundations.[5] However, on the way from Kant to Derrida, from Schleiermacher to Baudrillard, hermeneutics has been repositioned.

5. See Fredric Jameson, *The Seeds of Time* (New York: Columbia Univ. Press, 1994), pp. 8-21.

Hermeneutics is now positioned as fully the *power* of reading. Not simply the reading *of power* present in social, political, and cultural structure, the act of reading itself already displays profound and profoundly multidirectional, multivalenced commitments, even a tradition and its embodiment in the reader himself or herself. Reading itself is interpretation; it is a kind of writing. Reading therefore opens up the possibility of naming a poor writing, a poor interpretation. Reading then may be guided and directed toward truth. Of course, it is exactly at this point that our hermeneutic endeavors "expose themselves" as a more contingent and dangerous exercise than modernity had allowed and that postmodernity has yet to grasp. This is indeed what was anticipated in the rebellion of interpretation noted in the Reformation. Reading the text (in the Reformation case, the text being Scripture) already necessitates a right (correct) way of reading.

We could take our cues from John Calvin, who in his *Institutes of the Christian Religion* establishes a way of reading that shapes the way Christians understand Scripture. The crucial and fascinating factor is that Calvin is forced into a strange kind of polemic in the *Institutes* and in his commentaries. He has to argue for an epistemological priority of the Scriptures over the church. This is due to attacks by his enemies, who rooted the authority of the Scriptures exactly in the authority of the church. Calvin argued that they simply wanted to use the church as a foil through which they would have a kind of *will to power.* In the *Institutes,* he notes this:

> Thus these sacrilegious men, wishing to impose an unbridled tyranny under the cover of the church, do not care with what absurdities they ensnare themselves and others, provided they can force this one idea upon the simple-minded: that the church has authority in all things. . . . Again, to what mockeries of the impious is our faith subjected, into what suspicion has it fallen among all men, if we believe that it has a precarious authority dependent solely upon the good pleasure of men![6]

Exposing this evil cunning, Calvin then responds with the truth of the matter: the church, knowing that it is built upon the Scriptures, recognizes its God in them, and then venerates these words. Through Scripture, doctrine is formed. The truth of the Scriptures is yet to be recognized by the unbeliever. Calvin understands this problem to be addressed in two

---

6. John Calvin, *Institutes of the Christian Religion,* ed. John T. McNeill, trans. Ford Lewis Battles, 2 vols. (Philadelphia: Westminster Press, 1960), p. 75.

ways that stand in continuity. One way would be by unbelievers respecting the authority of the church. This would be an introduction, a preparation for faith. But the primary way in which the truth and credibility of the Scriptures are established is by the inner (secret) testimony of the Spirit to the reader — that is, the one who hears the words read or who reads them herself.

> The testimony of the Spirit is more excellent *than all reason*. For as God alone is fit witness of himself in his Word, so also the Word will not find acceptance in men's heart before it is sealed by the inward testimony of the Spirit. The same Spirit, therefore, who has spoken through the mouths of the prophets must penetrate into our hearts to *persuade us* that they faithfully proclaimed what had been divinely commanded.[7]

Calvin's signifying of the Spirit is multilayered. The Spirit is with the word and comes to the hearts of those who would believe. The Spirit is above human rationalities and the church itself but works through the church and through the words spoken by the servants of God. The result of the Spirit's work and the sign of the Spirit's presence, for Calvin, is belief in the words of the Scripture. Reading of the Scriptures is an act of prayer; it is, in a sense, praying the Scripture. What separates the fool and heretic alike from the true believer is that the latter reads aright and that reading aright is the result of the Spirit's *testimonium,* birthed in us in and through the church's prayers for our illumination and our own prayers for illumination.

Of course the credibility of that reading depends upon the judgment of the church, as Calvin tells us.[8] He leaves open the possibility that anyone can read and discover the truth of the Scriptures. Yet by challenging the ecclesial action of delineating the possibilities of right interpretation with another ecclesial action of delineating the possibilities of right interpreters, Calvin, like the other Reformers, opened a line of thinking that has come down through the generations, growing in power with modernity's shift to the subject in interpretation.

Modernity's shift to the subject, however, was not a shift to the fragility or vulnerability of the subject as interpreter. That was left up to postmodernity. Postmodernity's hermeneutic move can be characterized by the ques-

7. Calvin, *Institutes,* p. 79 (emphasis added).
8. Calvin, *Institutes,* pp. 69-92.

tion "Why should I believe what *you* say about a particular text?" Behind this question lie the real possibilities of a right reading, but that right reading will arise either from the *testimonium Sancti Spiritu,* the testimony of the Holy Spirit (if you are a Christian) or it will arise from *Creatio ex Nihilo,* out of nothing (if you are a Nietzschean in these matters, as are most "authentic" postmoderns). For the postmodern "interpreter," reading is the game and writing is the goal. Interpretation is only the writing of "my reading" inscribed by desire and now powerfully convincing because it is written. Convincing me is playing with me — serious play but play nonetheless. The "playful" character of reading is rooted in its creation out of nothing. For the postmodern, every reading comes from nowhere and is coming at them — a powerful advertisement.

So on the one hand, some people seek a conventional reading rooted in the conventional understanding of certain semantical and syntactical arrangements with a tradition of stable meaning, while on the other hand, some believe that they see a liberation in the emancipation of hermeneutics from the author. As Foucault reminds us, the death of the author is the resurrection of play and the possibilities of new life lived in the text.[9] Yet *playing* while reading has always been with us, but simply not as an occasion of liberation. Playing with the text is what the religious leaders did in Jesus' own day, who in their reading did not realize that the texts spoke of him. But to realize that the text speaks of Jesus is possible only with prayer. Because without prayer Jesus himself would be seen as *playing* with the text.

> And the Father who sent me has himself testified on my behalf. You have never heard his voice or seen his form, and you do not have his word abiding in you, because you do not believe him whom he has sent. You search the scriptures because you think that in them you have eternal life; and it is they that testify on my behalf. Yet you refuse to come to me to have life. (John 5:37-40, NRSV)

Reading biblical or social texts as playing or praying is now the heart of the matter. But a simple retreat into a tradition of reading with guaranteed stable meanings will no longer do. Again the question: "Why should I believe what *you* say about a particular text?" This is the postmodern question pressed upon us. Reading must [again] become praying. "Believe

---

9. See Thomas Flynn, "Foucault's Mapping of History," in *A Cambridge Companion to Foucault,* ed. Gary Gutting (Cambridge: Cambridge Univ. Press, 1994), pp. 28-46.

what I say about the text because you pray as I do, to the same God for mercy and justice and peace." Of course, this will not give us enough stability in our reading. Play is still a temptation, but where will yielding to temptation lead? The point that we must be reminded of is this: *The place of reading is a dangerous place and we must be reminded of the danger of reading.* Its danger stands near the place of knowledge and the demand for intimacy pressed upon us by knowledge itself.

The Intimacy of Knowledge and the Place of Truth: Knowing Begets Knowledge Begets Truth

Much Christian confusion over postmodernity can be traced to our failure to discern the sign(s) of the times. Confused interpreters lump together cultural diversity, pluralism, and relativism with the practices of canon formation and deformation, with the current formation and reformation of the disciplines, and even with the production, reproduction, and fragmentation of knowledge.[10] All of these ideas and practices are lumped together into single current events, events that anticipate in the minds of many some kind of approaching social and cultural Armageddon. These things could be understood as related but not the same and certainly not co-extensive.

More important, behind this lumping is an intellectual and existential fatigue born out of the attempt to resist the reframing of knowledge itself. As Lyon notes, "The very idea of privileged knowledge becomes nonsensical and the plurality of interpretations taken for granted. Becoming is all." For his part Lyon confesses the sin of sociology — it is a discipline that defines *determines,* and if it determines it then helps to reproduce "the thing" it defines.[11] Our participation in knowledge was suggested by the voices of modernity, but now the voices of postmodernity have found in that participation dirty, even bloody, hands. One has only to feel the sting of retribution for transgressing the boundaries of academic and theological disciplines to know that someone has hidden the weapons of warfare deep

10. See, e.g., David F. Wells, *No Place for Truth, or, Whatever Happened to Evangelical Theology?* (Grand Rapids: Eerdmans, 1993).

11. See Ben Agger, *Socio(onto)logy: A Disciplinary Reading* (Urbana, Ill.: Univ. of Illinois Press, 1989), p. 61.

within these channels of "knowledge." The disciplines as the organs and organizers of power and knowledge are slow, sweet temptations to believing in an ordered world with its clean and neat theoretical spaces.[12]

Of course, few postmoderns are unaware of this, nor do they fail to offer incessant critique and constant vigilance against the totalization of knowledge and the confidence placed in the structures of knowledge. More significantly, though, few if any postmoderns would trust anyone with any knowledge. That is to say, according to the postmodern critique, moderns showed themselves to be "poor stewards" of knowledge, choosing to use knowledge for power: the power to exclude, to judge unrighteous judgment, to establish and reestablish caste, class, race, and sex bias. Moderns have denied the use of knowledge for *intimacy* — to come to know and to love others. This is also to say that no one trusts anyone with any knowledge, especially knowledge of their own stories. How can women trust men with knowledge of their pain as women, or people of African descent trust people of European descent with knowledge of their suffering and even of their celebrations of life? Or how could Jewish people trust Christians with the knowledge of the Holocaust, especially given Christian participation? In this lack of trust is a powerful call *to know* in the biblical sense, to come and to love the cultural other as the basis of knowledge, which in turn will make sense of truth and of truth claims. This muted call to intimacy can be heard through the postmodern fragmenting of knowledge into knowledges and multiple canons of knowledge.

Thus sensitivity to the postmodern condition requires a rather new arrangement of knowledge and truth. Truth and knowledge are not the same. Rather knowledge must be seen as two realities. It is, first, intimate knowing, a *discernment* that leads to knowledge; knowledge then in this second sense is to be understood as the framing of discernment *in discourse*. Only then will this gaining of knowledge in both senses illumine truth. In the end, establishing a canon of knowledge and truth deposited in texts must issue out of love for humanity and must call forth love for all humanity. If it does not, then the legitimating of a canon will go wanting. Christians must learn that the defense of knowledge or the defense of established canons of knowledge is not always the defense of truth. But the defense of knowing is always the prerequisite to truth.

12. See Michel Foucault, "The Discourse of Language," in *The Archaeology of Knowledge,* trans. A. M. Sheridan Smith (New York: Pantheon Books, 1972), pp. 215-37.

The claim of and desire for intimate community must underlie the claim of truth. If community is missing, then the truth has become a lie and merely a sign of the chaos of power masked by the sublimity of order. Of course, many will find this deeply frustrating, and because of the fabricated symmetries of disciplines, their knowledges, their areas of sovereignty, their pedagogies become comfortable to those who have mastered them. These symmetries have not been unprofitable. But as much terrorism and violence have been hidden within them as have been discovered by them. This symmetry has also helped to conceal people in need of deep spiritual formation and healing, people with good minds, poor souls, and abused bodies. Knowledge must be transformed because knowledge without love can kill and often has killed. Yet, more important, knowledge with love will inevitably mean the transformation of the current symmetries of production, reproduction, and arrangement of knowledge.

A Hermeneutics of Retrieval: A Saving Death as the Birth of Community

How can one overcome postmodern suspicion? That it must be overcome is now the conclusion of many. For theologians, ethicists, cultural critics, scientists, and sociologists, what is at stake is the possibility of claiming "the real." All realists of whatever conviction understand that a real world, real social conditions, real human beings are positioned before them, standing in real need and calling for care and concern. This reality calls forth an ethic for postmodernity. What is needed, notes Lyon following Scott Lash, is a way of perceiving and being that "will not unendingly sweep away foundations but will attempt to lay open the ontological foundations of communal being-in-the-world." Yet like many other social and cultural theorists, Lash carries a deep "suspicion" of just about every form of communitarianism. Zygmunt Bauman, like Anthony Giddens, fears the colonization of social space by means of tribal or communal representation. In groups, we are always subject to moral manipulation and bifurcation.[13]

13. Zygmunt Bauman, *Postmodern Ethics* (Oxford: Blackwell, 1992), pp. 141-44; see also Anthony Giddens, *Modernity and Self-Identity* (Stanford: Stanford Univ. Press, 1992).

Our postmodern groupings are deeply arbitrary and lack a needed holistic moral compass. We stand now in the attempt by postmoderns to establish a moral compass that can be either a foundationless foundation in an a priori moral self or simply a morally arbitrary eclecticism that hopes to claim other postmoderns by means of rhetorical power. While others (most notably Bauman) seek a moral self, Lyon, much like John Milbank in *Theology and Social Theory: Beyond Secular Reason,* seeks a community of caring interpreters.[14]

The retrieval I want to argue for involves remembering the care spoken of in the Jewish and Christian Scriptures, connecting it with the ontological situation of communal being-in-the-world, and using this hermeneutically to interpret contemporary social situations and processes.

Lurking behind this beautiful desire, however, is a creeping voluntarism that is most likely Nietzschean in origin. For most postmoderns, even Christian ones, the will is a given. But it is exactly at this point that a hermeneutics of retrieval engaged in by "Christians of the postmodern" must recapture the secret of Christian community. That secret is the death of the will that brings life. All who become Christians are tempted to believe that it was their choice to become Christian. *They* said yes, *they* entered the Christian community, *they* chose this way of life, and *they* chose this God. This is *their* illusion that we allow them to keep until they come in — the self-deception we let them hold onto as a falsely firm foundation. Yet once "inside," once the flesh has been eaten and the blood swallowed, once baptism has been embraced and confession begun, a new reality comes into being. Once the songs of Zion are sung and the prayers spoken and heard, the truth can be heard. What is that truth? You had no choice. You were bound in sin and death and the false self. Your will was killed on a cross and new life began at an empty grave. And all this is by a Jewish man, the Messiah Jesus who has come and will come again. Thus an eschatological consciousness comes only with the death of the subject and of the will.

---

14. John Milbank, *Theology and Social Theory: Beyond Secular Reason* (Oxford: Blackwell, 1990), p. 389. "In my view, a true Christian metanarrative realism must attempt to retrieve and elaborate the account of history given by Augustine in the *Civitas Dei.* For one can only stick fast by the principle of 'intratextuality' — the idea that theology is an explication of the developing and rationally unfounded Christian cultural code — if one seeks for one's fundamental principle of critique within the Christian 'text,' and not in some universal and so foundationalist, principle of 'suspicion.'"

This consciousness rooted in the death of the self opens a door into a community that puts suspicion to death. Without this death, there can be no retrieval of life. Such a retrieval would baptize our own social gaze into the death of this man Jesus in order that we would see through his eyes and would see life. And in this seeing we would also see a city coming down from heaven and the old city passing away. We would see the evil that must be cast out and will be cast out of the social and finally hear the divine voice saying, Go in my name. Thus, in the last analysis, sociology and theology are not so different. They are bound together by a hope that the world we see will pass away and a new one will soon be born. This vision shapes the way I see things now.

Revelation and Human Understanding:
General and Special Hermeneutics

The Spirit of Understanding: Special Revelation and General Hermeneutics

KEVIN J. VANHOOZER

The Prodigal Interpreter: A Parable

"What Christianity gives the world is hermeneutics." Martin Buber's remark is both provocative and ambiguous. Is he saying that Christianity gives the world a *special* hermeneutic, that is, a method for interpreting the Bible in particular, or is he suggesting that *general* hermeneutics is somehow beholden to Christian faith?[1] My object is not to make a judgment as to what Buber actually intended, but rather to use his statement as a starting point for reflection. When Philip asked the Ethiopian eunuch if he understood what he was reading (Isaiah 53), the answer was "How can I, unless someone guides me?" (Acts 8:31). What exactly is the nature of this guidance, this extra "help" that goes beyond the reading of the words? Is it the guidance of tradition, community participation, the canonical context, or is it, in a sense yet to be determined, the guidance of the Spirit (John 16:13)?[2]

1. Hermeneutics is the "critical reflection on the practice of interpretation — its aims, conditions, and criteria." Charles Wood, *The Formation of Christian Understanding: An Essay in Theological Hermeneutics* (Philadelphia: Westminster, 1981), p. 9. "General hermeneutics" refers to those principles which govern the study of literary meaning as such. "Special hermeneutics" refers to those additional rules or principles that govern certain kinds of texts.

2. Both Philip with the eunuch and Jesus with the travelers to Emmaus interpret Scripture with Scripture. Berkouwer comments: "Understanding is not achieved by

131

For more than a thousand years, Augustine, not Philip, provided would-be readers with guidance. His *On Christian Doctrine* provided rules for biblical interpretation that served as the foundation of medieval culture. Despite its rich Christian parentage, however, hermeneutics has of late been squandering its inheritance. The prodigal interpreter has quit the house of authority in pursuit of Enlightenment autonomy. In the desert of criticism, however, his means of sustenance were eventually exhausted; famished for meaning, he wished to be called again. Now, giddy with freedom and hunger, he reads riotously, feeding off texts with no taste in a Dionysian, deconstructive carnival.

"Carnival" comes from the Latin (*carne valere* — literally: "to put away flesh [as food]") and refers to the custom of partying before the Lenten fast. The etymology is instructive, and the analogy with deconstruction is apt: the deconstructive carnival puts away the matter, the meat, of the text. It denies the presence of the Logos in the letter. Accordingly, it refuses nourishment from the text and remains in a state of perpetual fast; the feast — communion with the meat and matter of the text — is endlessly deferred. "Carnival" describes hermeneutics gone into the far country, where it has abandoned itself to deconstructive dissolution.

My strategy in what follows is twofold: I want to answer the question about how we read the Bible, whether with general or special hermeneutics, by looking at the debate between the Yale and Chicago schools, and to do so in the light of postmodern literary theory. By looking at one debate in particular, I hope to show hermeneutics in general the way back to its Christian home.

Theology undergirds our theories of language and interpretation. The Bible should be interpreted "like any other book," but every other book should be interpreted with norms that we have derived from a reflection on how to read Scripture. I stake my claim that the Bible should be read like any other book, and that every other book should be read like the Bible, from within a Christian worldview. Where does the Spirit fit into the process of faith seeking understanding?[3] Only the Spirit of understanding can

---

putting Scripture aside." G. C. Berkouwer, *Holy Scripture,* trans. and ed. Jack Rogers (Grand Rapids: Eerdmans, 1975), p. 112.

3. The idea that biblical meaning is something that can be recovered by understanding simply by reading relegates the doctrine of the Holy Spirit to the theological margins (so Francis Watson, referring to Richard Hooker, in Francis Watson, *Text, Church, and World: Biblical Interpretation in Theological Perspective* [Edinburgh: T. & T. Clark, 1994], p. 295 n. 5).

convict us of hermeneutic sin — that interpretive violence that distorts the text — and illumine our eyes so that we see the Logos that is "really present" in the letter. In the valley of the shadow of deconstruction, the best general hermeneutics may prove to be a *Trinitarian* hermeneutics. It remains to be seen, however, why I think the Spirit of understanding must be the Holy, rather than a secular, Spirit.

Theology and Literary Theory: Beyond Secular Hermeneutics

David Tracy is undoubtedly correct when he notes the pervasive influence of literary theory on theology.[4] I believe the reverse also to be the case: literary theory is bound up with the modification or the rejection of orthodox Christian positions. Secular literary theories are theologies or antitheologies in disguise.[5] There is good reason, then, to consider the hermeneutical character of theology as well as the theological character of hermeneutics.

In the first place, what is hermeneutical about theology? Theology is hermeneutical "since it deals with a tradition mediated in no small measure by written texts and their interpretation."[6] Here, however, the consensus ends.

Should we read the Bible "like any other book?" This is precisely what Benjamin Jowett contends, in his famous essay "On the Interpretation of Scripture" (1860). One of his primary concerns for reading the Bible critically was "to combat the obscuring of the true meaning of the biblical texts through traditional interpretations being forced upon them."[7] Reading the

---

4. "The influence of literary criticism and literary theory on Christian theologies has become a major factor in any reasonable interpretation or assessment of theology today." David Tracy, "Literary Theory and Return of the Forms for Naming and Thinking God in Theology," *Journal of Religion* 74 (1994): 302.

5. The allusions to John Milbank are intentional. Milbank argues that secular social theory is constituted in its secularity by its "heretical" relation to orthodox Christianity. John Milbank, *Theology and Social Theory: Beyond Secular Reason* (Oxford: Blackwell, 1990), pp. 1-3. I want to say the same of secular literary theory.

6. Werner G. Jeanrond, "Theological Hermeneutics: Development and Significance," in *Studies in Literature and Religion*, ed. David Jasper (London: Macmillan, 1991), p. 9.

7. Paul R. Noble, "The Sensus Literalis: Jowett, Childs, and Barr," *Journal of Theological Studies* (1993): 3.

Bible "like any other book" is the "master principle" for biblical interpretation. Two corollaries follow: one must pay attention to the historical context, and a text has only a single meaning, namely, the meaning it had for the original author.

Jowett spoke of the "diffusion of a critical spirit" in his time that inspired the interpreter to rise above theological and denominational controversies: "His object is to read Scripture like any other book, with a real interest and not merely a conventional one. He wants to be able to open his eyes and see . . . things as they truly are."[8] Critical interpretation would lift the fog of dogmas and controversies that have obscured the literal sense. The critical spirit, in recovering the original meaning, will cast out the "seven other" meanings that have taken up their abode in the text. The alternative to critical truth is ideology and illusion: "Where there is no critical interpretation of Scripture, there will be a mystical or rhetorical one. If words have more than one meaning, they may have any meaning."[9]

Stanley Hauerwas disagrees: "The Bible is not and should not be accessible to merely anyone, but rather it should only be made available to those who have undergone the hard discipline of existing as part of God's people." Fundamentalist literalists and liberal critics alike are "but two sides of the same coin, insofar as each assumes that the text should be accessible to anyone without the necessary mediation of the Church."[10] Jowett mistakenly believed that if interpreters only used the right tools they could attain the objective meaning and truth of Scripture. What is needed, says Hauerwas, are not scholarly tools but saintly practices: in order to read the Bible correctly we must be trained in Christian virtue.

Hauerwas challenges the "two dogmas of criticism" — that biblical scholarship is objective and that biblical scholarship is apolitical. First, against objectivity, Hauerwas argues that we cannot understand Scripture simply by picking it up and reading it "like any other book." Facts are not

---

8. Noble, "Sensus Literalis," p. 7.

9. Benjamin Jowett, "On the Interpretation of Scripture," in *The Interpretation of Scripture and Other Essays* (London: George Routledge & Sons, n.d.), p. 31. The interpretation of Jowett's essay has occasioned a lengthy debate between James Barr and Brevard Childs about what Jowett meant by "like any other book." See James Barr, "Jowett and the Reading of the Bible 'Like Any Other Book,'" *Horizons of Biblical Theology* 4 (1985): 1-44.

10. Stanley Hauerwas, *Unleashing the Scripture: Freeing the Bible from Captivity to America* (Nashville: Abingdon, 1993), pp. 9, 17.

just "there." What we see depends upon where we stand. The presumption that the Bible can be read "scientifically," with common and critical sense, leads to the second dogma, namely, that individuals can interpret and understand the Bible by themselves. Fundamentalists and biblical critics alike, says Hauerwas, "fail to acknowledge the *political* character of their account of the Bible. . . . They want to disguise how their 'interpretations' underwrite the privileges of the constituency that they serve." Truth cannot be known "without initiation into a community that requires transformation of the self."[11] Contrast Hauerwas's manifesto with Jowett's equally uncompromising position: "It is better to close the book than to read it under conditions of thought which are imposed from without."[12]

Hauerwas maintains that the whole endeavor to interpret the Bible "on its own terms" is vain nonsense. There is no such thing as the "real meaning" of Paul's letters to the Corinthians once we understand that they are not Paul's letters but the church's Scripture. It is the "sin of the Reformation," we are told, to assert *sola scriptura,* for this exposes Scripture to subjective and arbitrary interpretation. *Sola scriptura* is a heresy because it assumes "that the text of the Scripture makes sense separate from a Church that gives it sense."[13]

"Meaning" for Hauerwas is a matter of the use to which one puts the texts for the edification of the church. The obvious question, of course, is how the church knows what God is saying through the Scriptures if what God is saying does not coincide with the verbal meaning. Hauerwas here invokes the Spirit: "the Church, through the guidance of the Holy Spirit, tests contemporary readings of Scripture against the tradition."[14] A theological issue therefore lies at the heart of hermeneutical debate, namely, how does the Spirit lead the church into all truth? For Stanley Fish, a literary critic on whom Hauerwas depends, it is the reading practice of the interpretive community that produces the meaning. There is no such thing as the literal meaning for Fish. Similarly, for Hauerwas, the meaning that interests the church is not "the meaning of the text" but rather "how the Spirit that is found in the Eucharist is also to be seen in Scripture."[15]

---

11. Hauerwas, *Unleashing Scripture,* p. 35.
12. Jowett, "On the Interpretation of Scripture," p. 11.
13. Hauerwas, *Unleashing Scripture,* pp. 155 n. 7, 25, 27.
14. Hauerwas, *Unleashing Scripture,* p. 27.
15. Hauerwas, *Unleashing Scripture,* p. 23.

What is theological about hermeneutics? The answer comes into view when we trace the development of the so-called three ages of literary criticism. We can view their unfolding in terms of a downward spiral into a theological abyss, though there are signs that hermeneutics may now be returning from the far country.[16]

The crisis in contemporary literary theory seems to be a direct consequence of Nietzsche's announcement concerning the "death of God." According to Mark Taylor, "The death of God was the disappearance of the Author who had inscribed absolute truth and univocal meaning in world history and human experience."[17] For Roland Barthes, the disappearance of God leads to the death of the human author. The author's absence means that there is nothing that fixes or stabilizes meaning. The death of the Father-Author "thus liberates an activity we may call counter-theological . . . for to refuse to halt meaning is finally to refuse God."[18] As George Steiner puts it: "God the Father of meaning, in His authorial guise, is gone from the game."[19]

Interpretation is theological if it believes that there is something that "transcends" the play of language in writing. Derrida and Barthes are *countertheologians:* there is nothing outside the play of writing, nothing that guarantees that our words refer to the world. The loss of a transcendent signifier — Logos — thus follows hard upon the death of the author. The result is a textual Gnosticism that refuses to locate determinate meaning in the literal sense. Every truth claim is dissolved in a sea of indeterminacy. Hermeneutics has become the prodigal discipline, rejecting both the authority of the Father and the rationality of the Logos, squandering its heritage in riotous and rebellious reading.

With the death of the author and the rejection of the autonomous text, the reader is born.[20] Meaning is not discovered, but made, by the reader's rediscovered Nietzschian will-to-power. The text "has no rights" and "can be used in whatever ways readers or interpreters choose."[21] With

16. As I shall argue below, there are hints of a new turn to "Spirit."

17. Mark Taylor, "Deconstructing Theology," in *AAR Studies in Religion* 28 (Chico, Calif.: Scholars Press, 1982), p. 90.

18. Roland Barthes, "Death of the Author," in *The Rustle of Language,* trans. Richard Howard (New York: Hill and Wang, 1986), p. 54.

19. George Steiner, *Real Presences* (Chicago: Univ. of Chicago Press, 1989), p. 127.

20. Some critics have spoken of a "Readers' Liberation Movement."

21. John Barton and Robert Morgan, *Biblical Interpretation* (Oxford: Oxford Univ. Press, 1988), p. 7. Ronald L. Hall suggests that "the spirit of writing for Derrida is a

the birth of the reader, the divine has been relocated: the postmodern era is more comfortable thinking of God not as the transcendent Author but as the immanent Spirit.[22] The Shekinah cloud has settled on the interpreting community.

Ironically, it is largely nontheologians who have been calling, in current critical debates, for theological hermeneutics.[23] One of the most eloquent of these calls comes from a literary critic, George Steiner: "Any coherent account of the capacity of human speech to communicate meaning and feeling is, in the final analysis, underwritten by the assumption of God's presence."[24] Steiner makes a wager on transcendence; he has faith that what we encounter in language and literature transcends the mere play of signifiers. Logocentrism, for Steiner, is the basis for the covenant between word and world, the conviction that reality is "sayable." Steiner believes that the reader encounters an "otherness" that calls the reader to respond. There is a Word in the words, to which the reader is responsible. Of course, the sense of an other's "presence" in language may be only "a rhetorical flourish," as the deconstructionists say, rather than "a piece of theology."[25] If the appearance of presence turns out to be false, the result is a "deconstructionist and postmodernist counter-theology of absence."[26]

For Steiner, then, reading for the "other," for transcendence, is a theological activity. Interestingly, deconstruction also positions itself as defender of the other. Indeed, in Derrida's more recent works, the theme

---

demonic perversion of spirit. The spirit of writing is . . . a perpetual breaking, a perpetual sundering, a perpetual hovering, a perpetual play of signs. The spirit of writing is essentially disembodied, essentially a break with the world." Ronald L. Hall, *Word and Spirit: A Kierkegaardian Critique of the Modern Age* (Bloomington: Indiana Univ. Press, 1993), p. 178.

22. In his essay "Towards a Concept of Postmodernism," Ihab Hassan puts "God the Father" in the column of "modernity," and "Holy Spirit" under the category of the postmodern. Ihab Hassan, "Towards a Concept of Postmodernism," in *Postmodernism: A Reader*, ed. Thomas Docherty (London: Wheatsheaf, 1993), p. 152.

23. Umberto Eco worries about "overinterpretation" — the exaggeration of the rights of the reader over the rights of the text. *Interpretation and Overinterpretation*, ed. Stefan Collini (Cambridge: Cambridge Univ. Press, 1992), p. 23.

24. Steiner, *Real Presences*, p. 3.

25. See Graham Ward, "George Steiner and the Theology of Culture," *New Blackfriars* (Feb. 1993): 98-105. See the essays in Nathan A. Scott, Jr., and Ronald A. Sharp, eds., *Reading George Steiner* (Baltimore: Johns Hopkins Univ. Press, 1994).

26. Steiner, *Real Presences*, p. 122.

óf ethics — by which he means responsibility to otherness — has come to the fore. Steiner and Derrida represent, therefore, two very different ways — the one theological, the other countertheological — of doing justice to the "alterity" or otherness of the text.[27]

Which interpretive paradigm — which "theology" of interpretation — best guards the "otherness" of the text, its ability to say something that would confront and address us rather than reflect our own interests? Neither hermeneutics nor theology can afford to follow Ludwig Feuerbach's suggestion that what we find — God, meaning — is only a projection of ourselves. The hermeneutical equivalent to Feuerbach's suggestion that theology is really only anthropology is the view that exegesis is really only eisegesis. Such a strategy stifles transcendence and reduces the scriptural "other" to the cultural "same."[28] Deconstructive reading — insofar as it undoes determinate textual meaning — is violent. Instead of protecting the textual other, it tears it asunder by a kind of close reading that sometimes resembles harmless play but at others textual vivisection.[29] Only a herme-

---

27. More recently, several studies have suggested that Derrida is more appropriately associated with the tradition of negative theology.

28. Cf. Kevin J. Vanhoozer, "From Canon to Concept: 'Same' and 'Other' in the Relation of Biblical and Systematic Theology," *Scottish Bulletin of Evangelical Theology* 12 (1994): 96-124. Some have tried to counter deconstruction by reasserting the authority of the divine author. For Richard Lints, the Bible cannot be read like any other book, not only because it functions as Scripture, but because it has God as its author: "Certainly evangelicals can share with Jowett a concern for the original authorial intention in Scripture, but they must take care not to lose sight of the other half of the dual authorship or they will surely lose sight of the meaning." Richard Lints, *The Fabric of Theology: A Prolegomenon to Evangelical Theology* (Grand Rapids: Eerdmans, 1993), p. 75. What does divine authorship add? For Lints, it means that we should read each portion of Scripture in the context of the canon as a whole, for this is the appropriate context in which to consider the Bible as God's writing. Let me also note Lints's belief that, while God's meaning is never unrelated to the plain sense, neither it is limited to the plain sense (*Fabric,* p. 77). Charles Wood agrees: the claim that the Bible is the Word of God has functioned as a hermeneutical principle that instructs us to read the text as a unity. To read the Bible as Scripture, he claims, is to read the Bible *as if* it were a whole, and *as if* the author of the whole were God. See Wood, *Formation of Christian Understanding,* p. 70.

29. John Milbank believes that modern secularity is linked to an "ontology of violence," a worldview that assumes the priority of force and tells how this force (e.g., desire, energy, language, ideology, etc.) is best managed and confined — by secular reason. Christian theology, however, does not recognize chaos and violence as first

neutic that has cut its teeth on Scripture will be able to read for an understanding of the other. In what is to come, I shall defend the following thesis: the best general hermeneutics is a *theological* hermeneutics.

Yale and Chicago Revisited: Spirit and Letter

The discussion to this point has set a broad stage on which to rehearse the important debate between theologians at Yale and at Chicago over biblical narrative. If we speak of the "return" of hermeneutics to Christianity, to what home does it return? Where one locates biblical hermeneutics, whether nearer New Haven or Chicago, depends upon how one answers the following question: Should we read the Bible like any other book? If we should not, can we approach Scripture with a special hermeneutics without falling prey to fideism or relativism? The fate of the literal sense will serve as our litmus test as we attempt to deal with these questions.

For Hans Frei and the Yale theologians, the crucial issue is whether or not Christian theology and the biblical text are instances of a larger class — religion, text — and thus to be subsumed under general criteria of intelligibility and truth. Orthodoxy ultimately stands or falls on whether we can say that the Gospels are about the irreducible man Jesus Christ, or whether the texts are really about moral or religious truths of which Jesus is merely an illustration. Hermeneutics is inextricably linked to Christology. To put it baldly, nonliteral interpretation takes Jesus off the cross. The passion becomes something else than the story of Jesus. For David Tracy, on the other hand, the crucial issue is whether we can read for the literal sense in a way that is both faithful to the tradition and intelligible to people today. Whereas Frei bows the knee to the criterion of "Christian appropriateness," Tracy worships in the spirit of "contemporary intelligibility." In Chicago, the literal sense converses with the "lived sense" of human existence today.

---

principles. Only Christian theology is able to overcome nihilism. There is another way to think difference: not in terms of repression, but of reconciliation, of a peace that surpasses any totalizing reason. Christianity, says Milbank, "exposes the non-necessity of supposing, like the Nietzscheans, that difference . . . and indeterminacy of meaning necessarily imply arbitrariness and violence." *Theology and Social Theory,* p. 5. I shall develop these ideas in terms of hermeneutics in my reflections on the Spirit of understanding as a Spirit of peace.

Which of these two theological options best contains the resources with which, first, to do justice to the literal sense of the biblical text and, second, to withstand the onslaughts of deconstruction? This particular debate about the literal sense in biblical hermeneutics may serve to illumine the hermeneutical situation in general.

Like many other contemporary theologians, David Tracy, one of the foremost representatives of the Chicago tradition, wants to make the Christian faith intelligible in a pluralistic world. His strategy is to explain religion, the less well-known phenomenon, in terms of our experience of art, the more familiar. Works of art are true, not as accurate representations of the world, but rather as disclosures of some deeper truth about the world and ourselves. Both artistic and religious classics have the power to disclose certain existential possibilities, ways of seeing and being-in-the-world. Aesthetic experience becomes a general model in the light of which Tracy can declare: the Gospels are *like that*. Indeed, he can even claim that the truth claims of art and religion stand or fall together. Biblical interpretation is therefore a species of a much larger class.

How does the approach to theology and interpretation just sketched affect the literal sense? Like Rudolf Bultmann, Tracy believes that the literal sense objectifies God. God does not literally have arms and eyes. No, the real referent of the biblical narratives, namely, human existence, is metaphorical. What distinguishes the Bible from other poetic texts is not the way we read it, but the kind of possibility we find therein. For Chicago, religious truth is a matter of disclosing existential possibilities that can transform the life of the reader.

Frei, on the other hand, ranks criteria of Christian appropriateness higher than criteria of contemporary intelligibility. The prime directive of theology is to approach the object of its study — God's revelation and redemption in Christ — in an appropriate way. We must resist the "temptation of all theology" (Barth) to try to set out in advance the conditions for meaningful and true talk about God (e.g., natural theology) or about the biblical narratives (e.g., hermeneutics).[30] What good are universal criteria of rationality if one is trying to describe something as utterly and absolutely unique as the Christ event?

---

30. Karl Barth, *Church Dogmatics*, ed. G. W. Bromiley and T. F. Torrance, trans. G. T. Thomson and Harold Knight, 4 vols. (Edinburgh: T. & T. Clark, 1936–1969), 1/2, p. 4.

Historical critics like Jowett approached the texts with their own standards of intelligibility and truth. The natural world was more real to them than was the world of the biblical text. In order to "save" the text, they had to interpret it in such a way that they could accept it, namely, as a source for determining what actually happened. The critic did not trust the text as it now stands and so interpreted it to mean something else than what lay on the surface. Frei has brilliantly described how both conservatives and liberals eclipsed the biblical narrative. "Fundamentalism identified the grammatical and literary sense of a text with what the text's words ostensibly referred to."[31] They shared with biblical critics the urge to turn the literal sense into "a detective's clue to the discovery of [the historical] referent."[32] Some critics mistook the meaning for the historical referents behind the story; others mistook the meaning for the eternal truths above the story. In each case, however, the meaning becomes separable from the narrative itself. Biblical interpretation became "a matter of fitting the biblical story into another world . . . rather than incorporating that world into the biblical story."[33]

Frei looks to Karl Barth as a model of how to read the biblical narrative literally: "The universal rule of interpretation is that a text can be read and understood and expounded only with reference to and in the light of its theme."[34] Form and matter are inseparable. What the text says is what the text is about. Its meaning, in other words, is neither "behind" it, in history, "above" it, in myth or allegory, or "in front of" it, in the experience or world of the reader. In George Lindbeck's celebrated formula: "It is the text, so to speak, which absorbs the world, rather than

31. Hans Frei, *Types of Christian Theology,* ed. George Hunsinger and William C. Placher (New Haven: Yale Univ. Press, 1992), p. 158.

32. Hans Frei, " 'Narrative' in Christian and Modern Reading," in *Theology and Dialogue: Essays in Conversation with George Lindbeck,* ed. Bruce D. Marshall (Notre Dame: Univ. of Notre Dame Press, 1990), p. 152.

33. Hans Frei, *The Eclipse of Biblical Narrative: A Study in Eighteenth and Nineteenth Century Hermeneutics* (New Haven: Yale Univ. Press, 1975), p. 130.

34. Barth, *Church Dogmatics* 1/2, p. 493. Theological reading "is the reading of the text, and not the reading of a source, which is how historians read it" (Frei, *Types of Christian Theology,* p. 11). Understanding the text is an ability, a capacity "to follow an implicit set of rules unintelligible except in the examples of text . . . in which they are exhibited." Hans Frei, "Theology and the Interpretation of Narrative: Some Hermeneutical Considerations," in *Theology and Narrative: Selected Essays,* ed. George Hunsinger and William C. Placher (Oxford: Oxford Univ. Press, 1993), p. 101.

the world the text."[35] With regard to realistic narrative, we have the reality only under the narrative description.[36] We cannot go around, or behind, or over, or under the narratives to get to their subject matter; we have to go through them. Jesus is the literal subject of the Gospel narratives; the story is about him, not someone, or something, else.[37]

Tracy recognizes Frei's contribution in specifying the criterion of Christian appropriateness, the literal sense of biblical narrative, with greater precision. However, he cautions against privileging any one literary form of Scripture. We need to do justice to the plurality of biblical genres.

On Tracy's view, Christian tradition must be correlated with independent human experience in the world.[38] Frei's claim to self-referentiality is artificial; it disconnects the text from the extratextual world and from the process of reading.[39] In Francis Watson's words, "To regard the church as a self-sufficient sphere closed off from the world is ecclesiological docetism." Insights originating in the secular world can have a positive role in assisting the community to understand Scripture. The broader canonical context "suggests that the Spirit dwells within the created and human world as well

35. George Lindbeck, *The Nature of Doctrine: Religion and Theology in a Postliberal Age* (Philadelphia: Westminster, 1984), p. 118.

36. Frei, *Types of Christian Theology,* p. 139.

37. The realistic literal sense of the resurrection narratives, for example, is that the resurrection is a predicate of Jesus, not of the disciples. Bultmann is wrong to say that the resurrection stories are really about the disciples' coming to faith. Yet Carl Henry is wrong too if he implies that the resurrection is a kind of scientific fact. The notion of "fact" is as extratextual as Bultmann's category of "myth." The resurrection for Barth is neither myth nor history; the risen Jesus is neither a historical nor an ideal referent. What is the relation of the risen Christ in the text to history? Neither Frei nor Barth can specify the way in which the text refers to reality. The literal sense is a textual, not a historical sense. To put it another way, one can read the texts literally "and at the same time leave the referential status of what was described in them indeterminate." Frei, *Types of Christian Theology,* p. 138.

38. Tracy is not as pessimistic about the utility of general hermeneutics as is Frei. Tracy's own interpretation of the Gospels is *correlated* with, but not founded upon, his general hermeneutical analysis of the religious classic. David Tracy, "On Reading the Scriptures Theologically," in *Theology and Dialogue,* ed. Bruce Marshall (New Haven: Yale Univ. Press, 1992), p. 59 n. 16.

39. Frei was later to make this criticism of his own position. See Frei, "The 'Literal Reading' of Biblical Narrative: Does it Stretch or Will it Break?" in Hunsinger and Placher, eds., *Theology and Narrative,* p. 141.

as within the church, in which case truth may proceed from the world to the church as well as from the church to the world."[40]

These diverse criticisms raise the same fundamental query: Is intratextuality adequate for the full range of theology's task — for the church's mission to the world? The Yale school's strength is its clarification of the criteria of Christian appropriateness.[41] But that is only half of theology's job description. We need to engage the world in conversation about our theories rather than trying to hide behind our ecclesial skirts. Criteria of intelligibility are also necessary. Yet Yale remains suspicious of the terms of this conversation: general theories are Trojan horses. Existentialism may have made Paul's anthropology intelligible to certain twentieth-century thinkers, but in the end it chokes the Gospel within its own categories — a perfect illustration of philosophy capturing Christian thought (Col. 2:8).

What think ye of Christ? The Tracy of *The Analogical Imagination* might reply: "He is the manifestation of an always already possibility of an agapic mode of being-in-the-world." The literal sense is, on this view, dispensable. This is neither hermeneutically nor theologically appropriate to Christian faith, for the incarnation and resurrection are decidedly not members of a general class! Like Barth, Frei believes that we must begin with the particular. To begin with general categories is to risk swallowing up the act or the Word of God in a human conception of what was or was not possible. There simply is no nontextual access to the reality of Jesus Christ.

Yale has questions with regard to the suitability of Chicago's criteria of intelligibility as well. The community in which we stand does affect the way we read. We hear the Word when we participate in the form of life within which alone it makes sense. Furthermore, the reasons one gives for preferring the literal sense of the Gospel as one's basic explanatory framework are internal to the Christian tradition. So are *all* reasons that commend one's tradition, including the tradition of the Enlightenment. The only honest position to take in a rational conversation is to say "Here I stand." Tracy, however, tries to have it both ways: "Here I stand . . . and *there*."

---

40. Watson, *Text, Church, and World*, pp. 236-37.

41. "No theologian should deny that one major task of all responsible theology is to show how it is the tradition itself that is being interpreted and not interpreted away or invented." David Tracy, "Lindbeck's New Program for Theology," *The Thomist* 49 (1985): 468.

Tracy and Frei have qualified their respective positions in the wake of their confrontations in the early 1980s. Tracy has become less inclined to use a single conceptual scheme to interpret the Gospels; Frei became reluctant to define the literal sense in terms of realistic narrative. We might characterize the emerging position that has resulted from these peace talks as *canonical conversation in correlation with community context.* What new mutation of the literal sense does such a development represent?

In a recent article, Tracy agrees with Frei that all Christian theologians should acknowledge the plain sense as normative.[42] But Frei's emphasis on a unified coherent narrative overlooks the plurality and ambiguity within the canon itself. What theology needs is the full spectrum of forms in the Bible itself, with Jesus Christ the supreme "form" that informs all Christian understanding of God.[43] Neither modernity nor a unified narrative provides a general framework within which one can correlate religion and rationality. Tracy continues to believe that the project of correlation is indispensable. Conversation is the form rationality must take in the post-modern era. The interpreter converses with the ambiguous text and with the plural traditions of interpretation. Postmodernism calls for an ethics of resistance to all monologues, to all *isms,* that seek to close the conversation prematurely. Postmodern mystic readings identify God "as positive Incomprehensibility"; postmodern prophetic readings identify God as the one who acts in the cross of the oppressed and marginalized.[44] By identifying God as positive Incomprehensibility and as the one who is in solidarity with the suffering of the oppressed, Tracy seeks to preserve the literal sense of the passion narratives while at the same time going beyond it.

In his later work, Frei adopted a different strategy for preserving the

---

42. "Surely Hans Frei . . . [was] not wrong to insist that God's identity is Christianly established in and through the passion narrative's rendering of the identity of and presence of Jesus as the Christ." Tracy, "Literary Theory and Return of the Forms," p. 310.

43. David Tracy, "Theology and the Many Faces of Postmodernity," *Theology Today* 51 (1994): 111. Frei apparently conceded that Tracy might better fit into the third of his five types of theology. On this view, though Tracy would still wish to correlate the specificity of Christian faith with general criteria that would be culturally intelligible, he would do so in an ad hoc or piecemeal, rather than systematic, fashion. See Frei, *Types of Christian Theology,* p. x, for the suggestion that Frei became "fond" of Tracy, and p. 71 for a description of Type 3.

44. The principal biblical forms of naming God are the prophetic and the mystical. These are the two basic kinds of "further readings" of the plain sense. Tracy, "Literary Theory and Return of the Forms," p. 316.

particularity of biblical narrative from the hegemony of general theory. He focused on how the Gospels have been read by the church.[45] The proper context for determining the literal sense, he came to believe, is no longer literary, but sociolinguistic.[46] Literal sense is less a quality of the text than a function of community practice.[47] In short: "The plain sense is a consensus reading."[48] The inspiration for this approach is Wittgenstein, who urges us to look not for "the meaning" but to the use of a word or phrase. Frei applies this insight to the Gospel as a whole. The community consensus on Scripture thus becomes the stabilizing force for the notion of the literal sense. Frei finds that, throughout the history of the church, there has been broad agreement on two important matters: first, to take Jesus Christ as the ascriptive subject of the biblical narratives; and second, not to deny the unity of the Old and New Testaments. Any readings that do not violate these two conventions are permissible.[49]

45. The literal sense, Frei observes, is not one thing. See Frei, *Types of Christian Theology*, pp. 14-15. Just as its fortunes changed in the eighteenth century when it no longer meant "the sense of the text" but rather "the referent of the text," so it underwent a far-reaching (and fateful) change in his own work. Frei apparently dissociated himself from his earlier view on realistic narrative, even referring to it in the third person.

46. Not all of Frei's followers support him in this move (see Placher's comment). This may prove to be a significant breakup of a Yale consensus.

47. Frei began to speak of the "literal reading" rather than the "literal sense." He was influenced in part by his colleague David Kelsey's functional definitions of "Scripture" and by George Lindbeck's idea that the way religious language is used in the community is its normative meaning. For Kelsey, to say that a text is "Scripture" is not to predicate some property of the text, but to say something about the way the text functions in community. According to George Lindbeck, Christianity is a language game and form of life with its own logic. Understanding the Bible is a matter of participating in the Christian form of life. The meaning of a term, or of a text, is a matter of its use in a particular context. That is, neither words nor texts mean "in general," but only in specific contexts when used for specific purposes. Sentences do not correspond to reality in and of themselves, but only as "a function of their role in constituting a form of life . . . which itself corresponds to the . . . Ultimately Real." Lindbeck, *Nature of Doctrine*, p. 65. The correspondence that counts is not that between mind and thing, but self-in-action and God. The context that determines the meaning of Scripture is the church.

48. Kathryn Tanner, "Theology and the Plain Sense," in *Scriptural Authority and Narrative Interpretation*, ed. Garrett Green (Philadelphia: Fortress, 1987), p. 63.

49. The consensus covers the meaning of the stories about Jesus in an ascriptive mode, but not the reality status of the ascriptive subject Jesus. To put it simply, the consensus in Western Christian tradition concerns the literal sense rather than the literal reference of the Gospels. Frei, *Types of Christian Theology*, p. 143.

Two consequences attend this new definition: first, the literal sense is no longer a feature of the "text in itself," but rather the product of the community's interpretive practice.[50] It follows that there is no longer "any absolute distinction between the text's 'proper' sense and the contributions of an interpretive tradition."[51] No conflict between letter and spirit here: it is spirit, or community reading conventions, all the way down. Has Frei exchanged his hermeneutical birthright for a mess of pottage, or rather, Fish — stew? It was Fish, Hauerwas's muse, who first suggested that meaning is a product of the way it is read. It is the community, ultimately, that enjoys interpretive authority. Must all hermeneutic roads lead to Rome?

The second consequence of Frei's redefinition is a certain optimism with regard to the believing community. Interpretive might makes right. One may well question the grounds of such optimism: the believing community is all too often portrayed in Scripture as unbelieving or confused, and subsequent church history has not been reassuring either. If the literal sense is a function of community conventions, if there is no text in itself, how can we guard against the possible *misuse* of Scripture?

Tracy too now prefers to speak of "Scripture in tradition." The literal sense is the plain *ecclesial* sense. So long as the church gives priority to the plain sense of the passion narratives, other readings are permissible. Liberation and feminist theologians, Tracy assures us, have their own ways of maintaining "fidelity to the plain sense of the passion narratives." Even a "controlled allegorical exegesis" need not deprive the literal sense of its priority.[52] But what exactly does it mean to give "priority" to the literal sense, if this does not rule out multiple meanings, and especially if a pluralist like Tracy can now pledge his troth to the literal reading, too? What are the criteria for going beyond the letter? In ascribing authority to the interpreting community, both Tracy and Frei are relying on a theology, largely implicit, of the Holy Spirit.

---

50. Frei remarks that the "plain sense" — the consensus reading of Christian tradition — could well have been the "allegorical" rather than the "literal-ascriptive." That the plain sense happens to be the literal sense is a matter of an apparently arbitrary community convention.

51. Tanner, "Theology and Plain Sense," p. 64.

52. Tracy, "On Reading the Scriptures Theologically," pp. 49, 65 n. 64.

What Reformed Theology Has to Say
to New Haven and Chicago

I turn now to an explicit theological reflection on these two species of hermeneutical theology. What does Edinburgh — my location, my particularity, home of the Scottish Reformation and entry point of Barth into the English-speaking world — have to say to New Haven and Chicago? We can recast contemporary figures in Reformation roles: Tracy could play Erasmus; Frei, Luther; Jowett could stand in for Socinus; Lindbeck and Hauerwas could compete for the part of Menno Simons — and I shall take the part of Calvin. We can even cast Derrida, perhaps as a Ranter, or alternately, as representing the Reformers' untempered iconoclastic zeal. For what deconstruction does best is expose the sociopolitical and ideological interests surreptitiously at work in interpretation. At its best, deconstruction "calls me to be on guard against reinscribing the other in my image for my purposes."[53]

Truth: *Sola Scriptura*

In recalling Reformation debates, two themes are especially pertinent; first, *sola scriptura*. New Haven's insistence that "the text absorbs the world" seems to represent a "second coming" of the doctrine of *sola scriptura*. Absorbing the world into the text means ascribing primary truth to the literal sense of the biblical text, and interpreting all other experience in terms of that. New Haven has often been misinterpreted here. To say that the text absorbs the world is not necessarily to retreat into canon and commitment; it is rather a means by which the church can make public truth claims without first having to buy into some general conceptual scheme.[54]

---

53. Gary A. Phillips, "The Ethics of Reading Deconstructively, or Speaking Face-to-Face: The Samaritan Woman Meets Derrida at the Well," in *The New Literary Criticism and the New Testament*, ed. Elizabeth Struthers Malbon and Edgar V. McKnight (Sheffield: Sheffield Academic Press, 1994), p. 317.

54. Frei is willing to speak of reference and truth, but in each case, "it must be the notion of truth or reference that must be re-shaped . . . not the reading of the literal text." Hans Frei, "Conflicts in Interpretation," in Hunsinger and Placher, eds., *Theology and Narrative*, p. 164.

Truth is textually mediated. Frei was right to insist that the concern for intelligibility can skew one's reading of the plain sense of the passion narratives. Bultmann, for instance, had great difficulty satisfying simultaneously the criterion of Christian appropriateness and that of contemporary intelligibility. Indeed, his allegiance to both criteria generated the so-called structural inconsistency that debilitated his theology — no man can serve two masters.[55]

We can applaud Frei's dogged insistence that we have no independent access to the subject matter of the Gospels, without thereby sliding down the slippery slope of self-referentiality into Derrida's arms and the conclusion that there is nothing outside of the text. Frei's point is *not* that there is nothing outside of the text, but rather that there is no way that we can provide an independent description of its subject matter. The referent of the Gospels is Jesus, "not as someone to whom we may gain independent unmediated access but insofar as that historical person is mediated to us in and through the text."[56]

Sola scriptura means that Christians will view meaning and truth in a particularistic way. According to the philosopher Donald Davidson, interpreters seek to maximize the number of true sentences to a speaker's sentences in order to discover what they mean.[57] This is his so-called

---

55. On the notion of a "structural inconsistency" in Bultmann, see Schubert Ogden, *Christ Without Myth: A Study Based on the Theology of Rudolf Bultmann* (New York: Harper, 1961), p. 96, and Roger A. Johnson, *The Origins of Demythologizing: Philosophy and Historiography in the Theology of Rudolf Bultmann* (Leiden: E. J. Brill, 1974), pp. 15-18.

56. Watson speaks of Frei's "intratextual realism": the Bible refers beyond itself to extratextual reality, while at the same time regarding that reality as accessible to us only under the textual description. Watson, *Text, Church, and World*, pp. 224-25. The truth, then, is textually mediated, but it *is* a claim to truth. If we believe that the biblical narratives — our spectacles of faith — are the primary interpretive framework with which to interpret reality, then we must be prepared to meet challenges from other views. While we acknowledge that we see the truth from within and through the stories, we must continue to claim that it is the truth that we see. A retreat into narrative is not an option for a missionary faith.

57. Bruce Marshall believes that Donald Davidson's "truth-dependent" account of meaning provides a help to what Frei and Lindbeck are trying to say. See esp. Bruce D. Marshall, "Meaning and Truth in Narrative Interpretation: A Reply to George Schner," *Modern Theology* 8 (1992): 173-79. For an application of Davidson's theories to general hermeneutics, see Reed Way Dasenbrock, ed., *Literary Theory after Davidson* (University Park: Pennsylvania State Univ. Press, 1993).

Principle of Charity: interpret in such a way so as the bulk of the speaker's sentences can be considered true. In the seventeenth and eighteenth centuries, biblical critics began to ascribe centrality to another set of narratives in deciding about truth: modernity's naturalistic account of human history and religion. Accordingly, they interpreted the Bible in such a way as to make *its* sentences compatible with their new secular canon. Decisions about what is generally true thus shaped decisions about what the biblical text could possibly mean. Bultmann's demythologizing is the logical outcome of such "charity." In order to absorb the world into the text, however, we must ascribe primacy to the biblical narratives in deciding about truth and goodness.[58]

Perhaps the main function of *sola scriptura*, as Gerhard Ebeling observed, is that it preserves intact the distinction between text and interpretation.[59] Can New Haven and Chicago continue to do so? There is a real danger in tying the fate of the literal sense too closely to community consensus. Deconstructionists like nothing better than to dismantle dominant interpretations. To speak of a 1700-year-long consensus on reading conventions is virtually to beg to be "undone." Yale and Chicago now agree that what is normative for theology is "Scripture in tradition." Each affirms the priority of the literal sense, but Chicago wants to correlate it with what is intelligible in the contemporary context and Yale with what is appropriate in the context of the Christian community. Given their emphases on the uses of Scripture in Christian tradition, can they preserve the literal sense from corruption by the community, on the one hand, and from deconstruction, on the other?

58. Marshall observes, however, that according epistemic primacy to biblical narrative does not entail that Christians can never revise their beliefs in light of secular learning. The various reasons the community has for holding beliefs true are not incompatible with the function of Scripture to serve as the primary criterion for truth. "Dialogue with the adherents of other views of the world can give the Christian community compelling reasons to change its own established beliefs, without requiring it to surrender its identity by epistemically decentralizing the gospel narratives." Bruce D. Marshall, "Truth Claims and the Possibility of Jewish-Christian Dialogue," *Modern Theology* 8 (1992): 235. To take one example: the discovery of the Dead Sea scrolls may lead Christians to revise their interpretation of certain biblical passages. To do so is not to make one's allegiance to the literal sense of Scripture secondary, but rather to express one's allegiance to the text rather than to the tradition of one's interpretation of it.

59. Gerhard Ebeling, *The Word of God and Tradition: Historical Studies Interpreting the Divisions of Christianity*, trans. S. H. Hooke (Philadelphia: Fortress, 1968), p. 136.

The Yale school uses broadly Wittgensteinian arguments for locating meaning in community use rather than in some alleged reference. Let us assume that this account of meaning is broadly correct. Does it follow that what theologians should describe is the use of Scripture *today* rather than the use to which words and sentences were put by those responsible for the final form of the biblical text? To replace *sola scriptura* by "Scripture in tradition" — which is to say, by community conventions — is to use the wrong strategy at the worst time. We live in an age where deconstruction is exposing, and exploding, social conventions. The masters of hermeneutic suspicion excel in showing that what is mistakenly thought to be "natural" is merely "conventional"; this goes for the plain, "natural" sense of Scripture, too. Furthermore, we interpret in an environment strewn with cognitive pollution and subject to ideological pressures. Alvin Plantinga argues that human cognitive capacities have a design plan that specifies their proper functions, and he rightly observes that there is a difference between *normal* functioning and *proper* functioning.[60] I see no reason why cognitive malfunction could not be corporate as well as individual.

The interpreter has, it is true, an elder brother, the Christian tradition.[61] Individuals always read in some interpretive community. Perhaps the wisdom of the tradition exercises a moderating effect on readers today? Yet elder brothers, as everyone knows, can occasionally be bullies. The Council of Trent used 2 Peter 1:20 ("No prophecy of Scripture is a matter of one's own interpretation") to justify the church's right "to judge regarding the true sense and interpretation of holy Scriptures."[62] The Spirit of understanding is shut up here in a hierarchical interpretive institution.

The suggestion that community convention is of hermeneutic significance goes back further than Yale, or even Wittgenstein. It has at least one Reformation precedent. John Yoder draws attention to the novelty of the Anabaptist idea that "the text is best understood in a congregation." He points out that Zwingli appealed to 1 Corinthians 14:29 to make the point:

---

60. Proper function is a matter of our design plan; normal functioning is a matter of statistics. Alvin Plantinga, *Warrant and Proper Function* (Oxford: Oxford Univ. Press, 1993), pp. 199ff.

61. I borrow this analogy from Karl Barth.

62. Cited in Berkouwer, *Holy Scripture*, p. 115. Calvin, in his commentary on 2 Peter, takes this verse as a warning against arbitrary interpretation. Nothing in the context suggests that the point was to draw a contrast between individual and community.

"the Spirit is an interpreter of what a text is about only when Christians are gathered in readiness to hear it speak."[63] This is not the general Wittgenstein point about meaning as use but rather the Pauline point about understanding as discipleship. The Anabaptist hopes for something like Habermas's ideal speech situation, in which all those engaged in dialogue about what the text means now in concrete terms would, without coercion, discover unanimity. The final outcome of the conflict of interpretations would be reconciliation: "It seemed good to the Holy Spirit and to us."[64]

Can the church, empowered by the Spirit who leads us into all truth, ever go beyond *sola scriptura?* Some Anabaptists, like Thomas Müntzer, went too far in their pneumatic exegesis, claiming that the Spirit of understanding goes beyond what the written Word says. Does Frei's emphasis on community consensus similarly bypass the letter? Can the community ever "correct" the canon, say, for its position on women, or slavery? Can readers resist the literal meaning if it is oppressive? On the new view from Yale, "whether a text is experienced as contrary to the gospel is determined not only by its objective content but also by the way it is understood in the community."[65] But is it the interpretation or the text that is oppressive? My worry about defining the literal sense in terms of community practice is that we risk losing precisely this distinction between literal sense and community reading.[66]

Kathryn Tanner, a second-generation Yale theologian, has tried to reconcile the traditional emphasis on the integrity of the "plain sense" with Frei's emphasis on habits of reading. Tanner defines the plain sense as what an individual would naturally take the text to be saying "insofar as he or she has been socialized in a community's conventions for reading that text

63. John Yoder, "The Hermeneutics of Anabaptists," in *Essays on Biblical Interpretation: Anabaptist-Mennonite Perspectives,* ed. Willard M. Swartley (Elkhart, Ind.: Institute of Mennonite Studies, 1984), p. 21.

64. Cited in Yoder, "Hermeneutics of Anabaptists," p. 24.

65. Watson, *Text, Church, and World,* p. 235.

66. Barth is the paradigm for the claim that coherence with Scripture is the primary criterion of truth for Christian theology. According to Marshall, "scripture is rightly used as a test for truth only when it is read in a certain way." Marshall, "Truth Claims and the Possibility of Jewish-Christian Dialogue," p. 235. However, Marshall notes that for Barth the right way is the way that accords with the text. It appears that, while the Yale school continues to follow Barth's view of theology as a form of Christian self-description, they have departed from Barth insofar as what is described is a habit of reading rather than the text itself.

as scripture."[67] Textual sense is not "plain" in and of itself, but only to those who have learned specific habits of reading. But these habits are not themselves the plain sense. The community usually identifies the plain sense with "the verbal sense," or "the sense God intended." Community consensus, in Tanner's scheme, is only the formal, not the material, principle of the plain sense. Our ability to distinguish between text and interpretation, between the literal sense and the way it is conventionally read, ultimately hinges on this fragile conceptual distinction. Tanner insists that this distinction derives not from general hermeneutics, but from a particular convention of community practice. Thus the formal principle of the literal sense — the one that gives the text priority over subsequent interpretation — is grounded in a community habit, and the material sense, which specifies the nature of the literal sense, is indeterminate. There is an irony here: Frei began his defense of the literal sense by decrying the bad reading habits into which critics had fallen at the Enlightenment. To tie the literal sense to community habits seems peculiarly inappropriate in an age when consensus is an endangered species and when many readers have fallen into bad habits.

Of course, what I am calling "social conventions" could be described by New Haven as the Spirit's guidance. It remains unclear whether the Spirit may lead the church into new interpretations that go beyond the letter.

Trinitarian Hermeneutics: Word and Spirit

"He will guide you into all truth." (John 16:13)

How then does the Spirit relate to the literal sense?[68] This question lies at the heart not only of the skirmish between Yale and Chicago, but also of the larger cultural wars that blight the late modern era. The Reformers' notion of the relation between Word and Spirit clarifies the nature of the

---

67. Tanner, "Theology and Plain Sense," p. 63.

68. A number of recent studies have begun to explore the hermeneutical significance of the Holy Spirit. An early statement of this interest comes from A. J. Mac-Donald: "The Spirit's function is to teach, remind, guide, witness, glorify — surely all functions of a sustained process of interpretation whereby that which has been revealed by the Word . . . is made plain to men." A. J. MacDonald, *The Interpreter Spirit and Human Life* (London: SPCK, 1944), p. 118.

literal sense as well as Steiner's notion that there is a "real presence" in the text. Only a Trinitarian hermeneutics will meet the challenge put to interpretation by the massive a-theology of contemporary literary theory.[69]

First, to whom does the Spirit bear witness? Unlike traditional Roman Catholicism, on the one hand, where the Spirit is endowed to the church, and enthusiasm, on the other, where the Spirit is independent of both Word and church, Protestants affirm the Spirit's witness to individuals and community alike.[70] The apostle Paul writes that "those who are unspiritual do not receive the gifts of God's Spirit" (1 Cor. 2:14).[71] Gordon Fee comments that the Spirit is thus "the key to everything" — to Paul's preaching, to the Corinthians' conversion, "and especially their understanding of the content of his preaching to be the true wisdom of God."[72] This view of the Spirit's work gives a theological underpinning to Yale's emphasis on community practice. Frei concurs: "When Christians speak of the Spirit as the indirect presence now of Jesus Christ . . . they refer to the church."[73] Pneumatology becomes the crucial doctrine in describing whether special revelation needs a special hermeneutic. It also lies behind the Yale-Chicago debate over the possibility of correla-

---

69. A complete response is beyond the limits of this present discussion. Elsewhere I have developed Barth's threefold analysis of divine revelation in terms of communicative action. God, the Author-Father, is the agent of the act; God, the Logos-Word, is the communicative act; God, the Spirit-Hearer, is the communication of the Author's Word. Only some such trinitarian analysis can respond, I believe, to the death of the author and the loss of determinate meaning — the "counter-theology" of Barthes and Derrida. For a fuller presentation of these ideas, see Kevin Vanhoozer, "God's Mighty Speech Acts: The Doctrine of Scripture Today," in *A Pathway into the Holy Scripture*, ed. P. E. Satterthwaite and D. F. Wright (Grand Rapids: Eerdmans, 1994).

70. See George S. Hendry, *The Holy Spirit in Christian Theology* (London: SCM, 1957), chap. 3.

71. According to Gordon Fee, what it is that only spirit-filled people understand is the Gospel — God's salvation through the crucified One — the wisdom of God. See Fee, *God's Empowering Presence: The Holy Spirit in the Letters of Paul* (Peabody, Mass.: Hendrickson Publishers, 1994), pp. 102-3.

72. Fee, *God's Empowering Presence*, p. 104.

73. Hans Frei, *The Identity of Jesus Christ: The Hermeneutical Bases of Dogmatic Theology* (New Haven: Yale Univ. Press, 1974), p. 157. Fee similarly observes that the Spirit is the Spirit of the whole body of Christ. Fee, *God's Empowering Presence*, chap. 15.

tion. Must we limit the spirit of understanding only to the community of faith?

Tracy argues that general human experience is a proper test of Christian tradition insofar as God is present, as Spirit, in *creation* as well as in the community of the redeemed. True, some passages indicate that the Spirit "was not" until Jesus was glorified (John 7:39) and that the world "neither sees him nor knows him" (John 14:17); yet the broader canonical context may suggest "that the Spirit dwells within the created and human world as well as within the church."[74] Is there perhaps a general, as well as a specific, witness of the Spirit? For Tracy, the Spirit is less a consequence of the historical work of Christ than a universal of creation.[75]

Does New Haven unnecessarily confine the Spirit to the church by making the Spirit's work a function of community reading practices?[76] According to Stephen Stell, in an article that tries to move beyond Yale and Chicago, the identity of Jesus Christ is defined not only by the narrative framework of the Gospels "but also by particular experiences in our current

74. Watson, *Text, Church, and World*, p. 237. Watson also appeals to John Owen's claim that the Spirit works "in things natural, civil, moral, political and artificial" (cited on p. 239).

75. David Tracy, *The Analogical Imagination: Christian Theology and the Culture of Pluralism* (New York: Crossroad, 1981), p. 386. Stephen L. Stell says that in Tracy's account "the specificity of God's historical work in Jesus Christ is compromised by its transposition into the universal interpretive framework of created existence. And consequently, the work of the Spirit in revealing the proper interrelationships of the triune God . . . and the proper interconnections of God's activity among humanity . . . is effectively precluded." Stephen L. Stell, "Hermeneutics in the Theology and the Theology of Hermeneutics: Beyond Lindbeck and Tracy," *Journal of the American Academy of Religion* 61 (1993): 691. I made a similar criticism against Paul Ricoeur, arguing that Ricoeur systematically excludes the Spirit from his hermeneutics by consigning the power of appropriating and applying the text to the human imagination. See Kevin Vanhoozer, *Biblical Narrative in the Philosophy of Paul Ricoeur: A Study in Hermeneutics and Theology* (Cambridge: Cambridge Univ. Press, 1990), chap. 9, esp. pp. 248-57.

76. According to Lindbeck, the internal witness of the Spirit is restricted to "a capacity for hearing and accepting . . . the true external word." Lindbeck, *Nature of Doctrine*, p. 34. Stell notes the oddity of this position, maintaining uneasily as it does both that the Spirit has meaning only *within* the cultural-linguistic framework of the church, and that the Spirit's work is *outside of* the church insofar as it consists in encountering and enabling those who are outside of the church to "hear." Stell, "Hermeneutics in the Theology and the Theology of Hermeneutics," pp. 691-92.

existence."[77] Jesus' story does not end with resurrection but with Pentecost, the birth of the church. The authoritative story that identifies Jesus as the Christ is thus the one that is continued by the church, in the power of the Spirit.[78] Because the story is ongoing, Stell argues that the tradition, the community's use of Scripture, and thus the literal sense, are all alike open to creative transformation. Theological interpretation requires three elements working in cooperation: common human experience founded on God's work in creation, the Christian tradition grounded on God's covenant faithfulness, and creative insight into the divine life drawn from the guiding of the Holy Spirit. Biblical interpretation that is intelligible, appropriate, and inspired demands the cooperation of all three factors. Experience must be creatively interpreted and challenged by tradition; tradition must be creatively interpreted and challenged by human experience; creative insight must be challenged and interpreted by experience and tradition. This is a powerful Trinitarian model. But is Stell right in associating the Spirit with the creative imagination? And what, in his correlation of tradition, experience, and imagination, has happened to the text, and its literal sense?

Discerning the Spirits: Hearing the Word of the Author

"To each of us the Spirit is a sword which cleaves open the stubborn and obscure passages, illumines the chambers of the mind so that dark and uncertain thoughts and conclusions become clear and effective, and supplies us with practical interpretation."[79]

I propose a different Trinitarian model, based on the notion of revelation as communicative action. The *Westminster Shorter Catechism* states: "The Spirit of God maketh the reading, but especially the preaching, of the Word an effectual means of convincing and converting sinners." The Bible will only be heard as God's Word (and thus interpreted as a coherent unity) if

---

77. Stell, "Hermeneutics in the Theology and the Theology of Hermeneutics," p. 695.

78. Milbank, *Theology and Social Theory*, p. 387. Stell believes that the hermeneutical deficiencies of both New Haven and Chicago are rooted in a theologically deficient understanding of the Holy Spirit. Stell, "Hermeneutics in the Theology and the Theology of Hermeneutics," p. 697.

79. MacDonald, *Interpreter Spirit and Human Life*, p. 157.

we are enabled to hear it as such by the Holy Spirit. The Spirit, says Barth, is the Lord of the hearing. Does it follow that the Spirit's witness changes the meaning of the text, alters the literal sense? The witness of the Spirit is connected with the effectual use of the Scriptures. Whose use? Not the variable use by the community of readers, but the normative use of the author's. The Creed says, after all, that it was God the Father who spoke by the prophets.

Let us consider Scripture as a species of divine communicative action, consisting of three aspects. First, the Father's "locution."[80] The words are the authorized words of the Father/Author. Second, the "illocutionary" dimension: what God *does* in Scripture is testify, in various ways, to Christ.[81] Finally, to return to the Catechism, we may best view the Holy Spirit's work as God's "perlocution," that is, as what happens as a *result* of speaking. For example, by stating something (an illocution), I may persuade someone (a perlocution). The Bible includes many types of communicative acts and calls for a variety of responses and appropriation. While a good "general" hermeneutical rule might be, "read for and respect the illocutionary point," this is not the end of understanding. For understanding includes a moment of appropriation. Either the Spirit of Christ absorbs our world into the text, or the spirit of the age absorbs the text into our world. The *filioque* thus has an important hermeneutic parallel: as the Spirit proceeds from the Father and the Son, so we might say that the perlocution — the efficacy of the speech act — follows from the speaking and the illocution. Or, to put it yet another way: application must be governed by explication; a text's literal sense — its *intended* meaning — should govern a text's significance — its *extended* meaning. This is, I believe, how Calvin and the Reformers understood the Spirit's illumination: the Spirit convicts us that the Bible contains God's illocutions and enables us to respond to them as we ought. The Spirit is the effective presence of the Word, or on my terms, the power of Scripture's efficacious perlocution.

What, then, is it to understand the Bible? As the Yale school has

---

80. God the Father is the one who *est locutus per prophetas* in former times, and who now speaks through the Son (Heb. 1:1-2).

81. "Illocution" is a term in speech-act philosophy that pertains to what one does in speaking: we can warn, promise, forgive, command, and so forth. The illocution is what makes a communication count as a particular kind of action.

pointed out, there are many "spirits" of understanding — historical, literary, sociological. The Christian understanding, however, is the one that *follows* the Word. "Following" has at least two senses. We can follow an argument, or an explanation, or directions, or a story. But the other sense of following is the kind that Jesus wanted when he said, "Follow me." The difference is, I think, one between explanation and application. The Christian is not a hearer only, but a doer of the Word. We can follow an argument yet disagree with its issue. All too often, interpreters never reach the stage of application. The meaning of the Bible's promises, warnings, commands, and so forth "lies plain before their eyes," but they are suppressed in unrighteousness. The most profound kind of understanding, however, has to do with the cultivation of the ability to follow the Word of God, not just in our reading, but in our personal response to what we have read. "One who understands a text will be able to make use of the text in ways that demonstrate — and in some sense constitute — understanding."[82] Understanding is our ability to follow the Word.

Understanding is theological because we are only enabled to follow the issue of the text by the Holy Spirit. The role of the Spirit is to enable us to take the biblical texts in the sense that they were intended, and to apply or follow that sense in the way we live. To use Gordon Fee's fine phrase, we might say that the Spirit is the "empowering presence" of the Word in the written words. The Spirit of understanding enlivens the church only when it is a church of the Word, and the Spirit enlivens the Word only when it is a Word in the church.

How shall we respond to the French Revolution in literary theory? Edmund Burke's *Reflections on the French Revolution,* two centuries old, proves surprisingly relevant and provides us with some starters. Like the earlier French Revolution, deconstruction is rife with the rhetoric of *liberté* and *égalité.* Burke spoke of the "confused jargon of their Babylonian pulpits" and warned that "learning will be cast into the mire, and trodden down under the hoofs of a swinish multitude." What moral might my mediation of New Haven and Chicago have for the hermeneutic revolution coming out of Paris?

---

82. Wood, *Formation of Christian Understanding,* p. 17.

Approaching the Other:
Understanding as Privilege and Responsibility

"Logocentric commentary . . . is docetic; it favors the spirit at the expense of the body of the text."[83]

Because interpreters are also sinners who suppress the Logos in unrighteousness, a certain amount of suspicion can be healthy. A *little* deconstruction may not be a dangerous thing. However, when deconstruction seeks to undo not only oppressive interpretations but the texts themselves, when it pries apart textual coherence for the sake of a repressed otherness, here I cannot follow. Deconstruction, far from protecting the text as an "other," licenses interpretive violence.

Deconstruction contradicts two basic principles of a Christian worldview: first, the "realism principle" (viz., we can adequately know the world and are responsible for doing so); second, the "bias principle" (viz., we never know the world apart from biases that influence our perception of reality).[84] Now apply these two principles to hermeneutics. First, the realism principle: we can adequately understand texts; second, the bias principle: we can never understand texts apart from biases that affect our understanding. The Spirit of understanding progressively convicts us of our biases and conforms us to reality.

Language does not bar us from reality, though reality comes mediated by language. Neither language nor finitude justifies interpretive sloth. Being indifferent to the text is not a way of doing justice to its "otherness." While we must be as honest as possible about our biases, they do not constitute an excuse not to interpret. Language, a gift of God, is adequate for the purposes for which it was created.[85] Babel is not a license for interpretive anarchy, neither does it warrant a despair of

---

83. Phillips, "Ethics of Reading Deconstructively," p. 289.

84. I am borrowing from Richard Lints, *Fabric of Theology*, p. 20.

85. Dallas Willard attributes to me the view that language is necessarily distorting. In fact, I am not in despair about language so much as about willful interpreters. I am not a framework-relativist. The problem is not finitude, but fallenness. The interpretive difficulties my discussion raises concern neither the social nor cultural positions of interpreters, but rather their moral and spiritual *dispositions*. The Spirit of understanding does not circumvent our finitude but renews, restores, and perfects our interpretive capacities.

language. The biblical text, taken literally, is an adequate testimony to Jesus Christ.

If the hermeneutics of conviction declares, "Here I stand," the hermeneutics of humility asks, "How does it look from where *you* stand?" The false humility of deconstruction degenerates into a despair of language and of our ability to interpret. True hermeneutic humility, on the other hand, is willing to receive something from the other, from the text, and from other interpreters. Does humility before the text rule out a critical moment in which the reader assesses its content? Am I advocating hermeneutic fideism: "Love God, and read as you please"? No, for understanding must be tested. Christian interpreters must endure every test that critics care to throw at them. Testing and enduring: these are signs of rationality and humility alike. Interpreters should never idolize their interpretations. I am seeking a degree of interpretive confidence somewhere between pride and sloth — the humble conviction that stands firm, even while acknowledging that it is rooted on earth rather than looking down from heaven. We do not yet have absolute knowledge. Yet we do have adequate knowledge, enough to respond to the overtures of the Word. Our first reflex upon being addressed should be one of trust. We must at least be willing to hear the other rather than drown out its voice, even when its message is a potential threat to our way of being in the world.

General or Special Hermeneutics?

Karl Barth and Paul Ricoeur are the two influential figures behind the Yale and Chicago schools respectively. Each has tried, in different ways, to reverse the hermeneutical reversal by making general hermeneutics a subset of biblical hermeneutics. We might paraphrase their strategies as follows: "Read any other book like the Bible" — a thought that neatly turns Jowett's maxim on its head. It is from just such an inverted position that we can, I believe, respond to deconstruction.

There is no such thing, for Barth, as special biblical hermeneutics. Nor is there an adequate general hermeneutics apart from biblical hermeneutics: "It is from the word of man in the Bible that we must learn what has to be learned concerning the word of man in general."[86] General

86. Barth, *Church Dogmatics* 1/2, p. 466.

hermeneutics is, therefore, a "predicate" of biblical hermeneutics. We begin with biblical interpretation and learn how to interpret texts in general. "Is it not the case that whatever is said to us by men obviously wants . . . to make itself said and heard? It wants in this way to become to us a subject matter."[87] What all speakers want, however, only the Spirit, as Lord of the hearing, can actually achieve. Buber's remark — "What Christianity gives the world is hermeneutics" — is not only a past fact but also a promise.

Just what is the role of the interpreter in understanding? Barth accepts the bias principle: "There has never yet been an expositor who has allowed only Scripture alone to speak." We must not think that any one interpretive scheme is particularly suited to apprehend the Word of God: "there is no essential reason for preferring one of these schemes to another." Barth then draws an astonishing conclusion: those schooled in biblical interpretation are best able to do justice to textual otherness: "Even from a human point of view, it is possible to regard scriptural exposition as the best and perhaps the only school of truly free human thinking — freed, that is, from all the conflicts and tyranny of systems in favor of this object."[88] Ricoeur agrees, insisting that understanding the other requires the reader to put oneself into question and to be ready to abandon one's self-understanding.[89]

This leads me to the following thesis: *All hermeneutics, not simply the special hermeneutics of Scripture, is "theological."* Does special revelation need a special hermeneutic? On the contrary, I am advocating a Trinitarian herme-

87. For his view of the literal sense, see Barth, *Church Dogmatics* 1/2, chap. 3, esp. pp. 464-72, 492-95, 715-36.

88. Barth, *Church Dogmatics* 1/2, pp. 728, 733, 735.

89. Like Barth, Ricoeur argues that biblical interpretation, which is prima facie an instance of regional or special hermeneutics, in fact overturns the very relation between general and special hermeneutics. The object of hermeneutics in general is to "unfold" the world of the text. Paul Ricoeur, "Philosophical Hermeneutics and Theological Hermeneutics," *Studies in Religion* 5 (1975/76): 25. The Bible is special because its world reveals my world in a new way, which forces me to abandon my old self-understanding. For Ricoeur, such revelation is experienced as a nonviolent appeal to the imagination. Theological hermeneutics thus qualifies general hermeneutics: all reading of poetic texts, insofar as they have the capacity to transform my existence, are potentially "revelatory." Ricoeur depicts a general hermeneutics that has been transformed by biblical hermeneutics. Note, however, that sacred hermeneutics has been secularized: the power of appropriating the world of the biblical text is attributed to the creative imagination, not to the Holy Spirit. See Vanhoozer, "Biblical Narrative in the Philosophy of Paul Ricoeur," chap. 9.

neutic for all interpretation; better, I am arguing that general hermeneutics is inescapably theological. Our polluted cognitive and spiritual environment darkens understanding — of *all* texts. Derrida is right to expose the many sources of coercion and distortion in the process of communication. Often we do not wish to understand the other, perhaps because the other has a claim on us, perhaps because we might have to change. Self-love can pervert the course of interpretation as it does every other human activity. It is the Spirit who enables us to transfer attention away from ourselves and our interests to the text and its subject matter. Understanding — of the Bible or of any other text — is a matter of ethics, indeed, of spirituality.

Indeed, interpretation ultimately depends upon the theological virtues of faith, hope, and love. *Faith,* that there is a real presence, a voice, a meaning in the text; *hope,* that the interpretive community can, in the power of the Spirit, attain an adequate, not absolute, understanding; *love,* a mutual relation of self-giving between text and reader. Abraham Kuyper contrasts our darkened understanding with love, the "sympathy of existence": "A lover of animals understands the life of the animal. In order to study nature in its material operations, you must love her. Without this inclination and this desire toward the object of your study, you do not advance an inch."[90] Kuyper's "principle of charity" is far removed from Davidson's, where we "love" the other by making it conform to what we think is true.

Non-Christian hermeneutics wreaks interpretive violence on the "other" of the text.[91] Deconstruction claims to be ethically responsible in reading for the "other," for all those things that do not neatly fit into our systems. Deconstruction, according to Gary Phillips, "calls me to be on guard against reinscribing the other in my image for my purposes."[92] I do not agree. Deconstruction does not serve the other. The message of the text is not allowed to "be" — the sense of the text is undone, doomed to wander like a shade through the rubble of signifiers that signify nothing. Deconstruction is a denial of the literal sense, a hermeneutic Gnosticism that claims to "know" the absence of the Logos.

90. Abraham Kuyper, *Principles of Sacred Theology,* trans J. Hendrick De Vries (Grand Rapids: Baker, 1980), p. 111. I am indebted to Nicholas Wolterstorff for this point. See Wolterstorff, "What New Haven and Grand Rapids Have to Say to Each Other," in *The Stob Lectures* (Calvin College and Theological Seminary, 1992–1993), pp. 28-30.

91. This is essentially John Milbank's thesis about social theory transferred to the realm of *literary* theory. See Milbank, *Theology and Social Theory,* part 4.

92. Phillips, "Ethics of Reading Deconstructively," p. 317.

The prodigal interpreter has need of theological virtues.[93] Faith, hope, and love alone enable us to avoid doing interpretive violence to the text. The fruit of the Spirit of understanding is peace — a letting be, a welcome reception of the other. The mention of peace and justice recalls the Anabaptists, who emphasized the role of discipleship and obedience in biblical interpretation. That we are able to surrender our self-interests and extend the "sympathy of existence" toward the text is a fruit of the Spirit.[94] In addition, the Anabaptists acknowledged a link between obedience and knowledge: "The readiness to obey Christ's words is prerequisite to understanding them."[95] If understanding involves obedience, it is easy to see how deconstruction could quench the spirit of understanding. According to Derrida, there is nothing "there" in the text to which we can respond. Deconstruction's vaunted ethics, which supposedly guards the otherness of the text from being swallowed up by dominant interpretations, ultimately founders in the absence of something determinate to which the reader can responsibly respond. There can be no genuine encounter if the interpretive community's practice creates the text. If the world of the text is the reader's projection, interpretation is only the repetition of the self-same and the same self. Contrast that vain repetition with C. S. Lewis's "taste for the

93. Dallas Willard wonders whether I have worked a hermeneutical variant of "occasionalism," a philosophical theory (largely discredited and associated with Malebranche) about the mind-body problem that maintains that mental intentions are coordinated with bodily movements only with divine assistance. In other words, it is God who puts together my intention to raise my arm and my arm's actual movement. Is it my position that the interpreter's understanding is only coordinated with the text thanks to divine assistance, that understanding a text is like raising my arm? The answer depends on what one means by "understanding." I agree that readers often can recognize illocutionary points without divine assistance. Humans are, I believe, created with the capacity to understand discourse. However, I also believe that this cognitive equipment has been affected by sin. It is often in the sinner's interest willfully to misunderstand or, at least, not to respond to what has been understood. If understanding involves a moment of personal appropriation, that is, if understanding includes the perlocutionary effect, then we can agree with Barth that the Spirit is the "Lord of the hearing." There are indeed some things we cannot do without divine assistance. We may be able to raise our arms, but we are only able to raise our arms in praise to God thanks to the prompting of the Holy Spirit.

94. Henry Poettecker, "Menno Simons' Encounter with the Bible," in Swartley, ed., *Essays on Biblical Interpretation,* pp. 62-76.

95. Walter Klassen, "Anabaptist Hermeneutics: Presuppositions, Principles, and Practice," in Swartley, ed., *Essays on Biblical Interpretation,* p. 6.

other": Lewis read to enlarge his being and to transcend himself. For the deconstructive critic who lacks the spirit of understanding the other, however, to read a thousand books is still to be alone with oneself.[96]

The Spirit of the Letter

To sum up: the Spirit of understanding is neither Jowett's critical spirit, nor Tracy's spirit of the age, nor Lindbeck's community Spirit, nor the rebellious spirit of deconstruction. I have argued that the Spirit of understanding is the Holy Spirit, the Spirit of Christ. The Spirit may blow where, but not *what,* he wills. The Spirit is subordinate to the Word. Perlocutions "proceed from" illocutions.

These other spirits are ultimately false spirits insofar as they devalue the letter — the Word of God written. They devalue the letter by emptying it of determinate meaning, depriving the text of any independent integrity and of the ability to resist the projections that critics foist upon it. I have argued that the Spirit witnesses to what is other than himself — to meaning "accomplished" — and that the Spirit enables readers to respond to this textual other — to meaning "applied." For the sake of clarity, we can distinguish three aspects of the Spirit's role in the process of interpretation.

First, the Spirit *convicts* us that the Bible is indeed the locution of God that bears authoritative witness to the living Word (and thus that we should view it as a unity).[97] Even this aspect of biblical hermeneutics has its secular counterpart, insofar as ethical interpretation means reading for the intent of the author.

Second, the Spirit *illumines* the letter by impressing upon us the full force of its communicative action, its illocutions. The Spirit does not alter biblical meaning. Rather, "the spiritual sense is the literal sense correctly understood."[98] The distinction between "letter" and "spirit" is just that between reading the words and grasping what one reads. Likewise, the

96. The original quote from C. S. Lewis reads: "In reading great literature I become a thousand men and yet remain myself." C. S. Lewis, *An Experiment in Criticism* (Cambridge: Cambridge Univ. Press, 1961), p. 141.

97. This is a restatement of the traditional Reformed notion of the "internal witness."

98. Charles Wood, commenting on Luther, in Wood, *Finding the Life of a Text,* p. 102.

difference between a "natural" and an "illumined" understanding is that between head and heart knowledge, between, on the one hand, having an opinion, and on the other, having a "deep sense of its truth, goodness, and beauty."[99] Illumination has to do with the quality and the force of our appreciation of the literal sense.

Third, the Spirit *sanctifies* us and so helps us to accept what is in the text instead of preferring our own interpretations. The Spirit progressively disabuses us of those ideological or idolatrous prejudices that prevent us from receiving the message. (This aspect of the Spirit's work is relevant for general hermeneutics, too). In so doing, the Spirit renders the Word *effective.* To read in the Spirit does not mean to import some new sense to the text, but rather to let the letter be, or better, to apply the letter rightly to one's life. The Spirit of understanding is the efficacy of the Word, its perlocutionary power. According to John Owen, the Spirit is the "primary efficient cause" of our understanding of Scripture. Yet the Spirit's illumining work is not independent of our own efforts to understand. "It is the Spirit's activity, effected through our own labor in exegesis, analysis, and application, of showing us what the text means for us."[100]

Two unresolved questions remain. First, we have seen that the relation between God's universal work in creation and God's particular work in the church is of no little hermeneutical significance. Is there some relation between human beings (as spirits) and God, other than that established in Christ?[101] In what measure is the Spirit of understanding outside of the church? Is biblical interpretation a work perhaps of common grace? The point to note is that all of these hermeneutical questions are properly theological as well.

Second, how can we recognize the Spirit of understanding? I must offer at least the outline of an answer to such an important query: we recognize the Spirit in those who confess that Jesus — the Logos — came in the flesh. Similarly, we recognize the Spirit of understanding in those

---

99. Fred H. Klooster comments: "The aim of Spirit-illumined interpretation should be heart-understanding," by which he means the worship and service of God. Fred H. Klooster, "The Role of the Holy Spirit in the Hermeneutic Process," in *Hermeneutics, Inerrancy, and the Bible,* ed. Earl D. Radmacher and Robert D. Preus (Grand Rapids: Zondervan, 1984), p. 468.

100. J. I. Packer, *Keep in Step with the Spirit* (Leicester: Inter-Varsity Press, 1984), p. 239.

101. Hendrey, *Holy Spirit in Christian Theology,* chap. 5.

who respond to the literal sense — to the commands, the promises, the warnings, the narratives — in a hermeneutically and Christianly appropriate manner. In short, we recognize the Spirit of understanding in those who "follow," that is, in those who hear, and do, the Word. "Those who would live under the authority of the Spirit must bow before the Word as the Spirit's textbook . . . those who would live under the authority of Scripture must seek the Spirit as its interpreter."[102]

The Homecoming of Hermeneutics

If hermeneutics were to return home to Christianity, this would indeed be cause for rejoicing. In anticipation of the homecoming of the prodigal, then, I wish to conclude with the image of a feast. We must remember to conjoin Word with sacrament as well as Spirit. The eating of Christ's flesh is a tangible reminder that an Easter feast follows our Lenten fast. Christians conduct this feast not in the spirit of carnival but in the spirit of communion: with Christ, and with one another. We may likewise celebrate the feast of interpretation. The Spirit of Pentecost overcomes the cultural and ideological biases that distort communication and so restores language as a medium of communion. Thanks to the Spirit of understanding, the letter of the text becomes an enlivening, and nourishing, presence. We now enjoy only the first-fruits of understanding, but we look forward to that day when we will understand as we have been understood. *Veni spiritus interpres!* Come interpreter Spirit!

---

102. Packer, *Keep in Step*, p. 240.

Hermeneutical Occasionalism

DALLAS WILLARD

In his intriguing essay on "The Spirit of Understanding," Kevin Vanhoozer takes the position that general hermeneutics, or the principles that govern the study of literary meaning as such, are not sufficient as a basis for the understanding of the biblical texts. Rather, a special kind of guidance, generally accessible to individuals within the faithful community, is required. This is the guidance of the triune God through the offices of the Holy Spirit. Guidance from the believing community is, for him, valid only insofar as it is an expression of the action of the Spirit: "There is a real danger in tying the fate of the literal [actual?] sense too closely to community consensus." And: "I see no reason why cognitive malfunction could not be corporate as well as individual." And: "The Bible will only be heard as God's Word . . . if we are enabled to hear it as such by the Holy Spirit." Further, the understanding of the Word is not something separable from the application of it in action. Application completes understanding. "The Christian understanding . . . is the one that *follows* the Word. . . . Understanding is our ability to follow the Word. . . . The role of the Spirit is to enable us to take the biblical texts in the sense that they were intended, and to apply or follow that sense in the way we live."

I am largely, if not completely, in agreement with the position that emerges from Vanhoozer's discussion. My intent is to raise some of the most difficult issues his type of position faces. To sharpen these issues quickly I shall use the phrase "hermeneutical occasionalism" as suggestive of both the content and the difficulties of the position.

167

Occasionalism, we recall, was a post-Cartesian interpretation of mind/body interaction, most strongly associated with the name of Nicolas Malebranche.[1] Under Descartes's descriptions of the mind or soul and the body, they were of distinct and separable essences. But being of such radically different kinds, how could they possibly interact? Of the numerous positions that developed in response to this question, some held that they did not interact but only ran parallel, while Malebranche and others thought that they did interact, but only indirectly. Without divine assistance they could not influence one another, but God could interact with each side in turn and thereby allow what happens in one realm to determine what happened in the other. For example, when the flesh in your foot is separated by a tack you step on, God takes note and produces a pain and other relevant phenomena in your mind. Or when you resolve to lift your arm, God notes this mental event and (through whatever mechanism) brings it about that your arm rises.

My hope is that the application to the hermeneutical situation will be immediately and intuitively clear. The problem is to get the (or a) *right* interpretation or understanding of the text — here, for simplicity sake, a biblical text. Vanhoozer seems to make authorial intent or use authoritative: "The witness of the Spirit is connected with the effectual use of the Scriptures. Whose use? Not the . . . community of readers, but the . . . author's. The Creed says, after all, that it was God the Father who spoke by the prophets." So getting the right interpretation or understanding of the text will be a matter of capturing for ourselves God's thought in expressing himself through the text in question.

Now, is it possible for us to achieve this if we are limited to the resources of unbelievers operating from within the relevant social/historical contexts, or even of all that plus the Christian community within which we live, however that is to be spelled out? I believe that Vanhoozer holds this to be impossible. Of course we must live among unbelievers and may also live in Christian community. But that will not be enough to allow us to achieve a right understanding of God's thought in expressing himself through a given biblical text, any more than, under the occasionalist view, the intent to raise my arm is enough to make it go up.

---

1. See Nicholas Malebranche, *The Search after Truth and Elucidations of the Search after Truth,* trans. Thomas M. Lennon and Paul J. Olscamp (Columbus: Ohio State Univ. Press, 1980). For a discussion of Malebranche, see Paul Hazard, *The European Mind, 1680–1715,* trans. J. Lewis May (Cleveland: Meridian, 1963), pp. 133-42.

. I suspect that in adopting this position Vanhoozer is accepting the view — fundamental to the entire discussion and far beyond — that the "cultural context" (most importantly the language, rituals, and cosmic assumptions of the respective group or groups) makes it impossible to determine "how things are in themselves." True, he states, and I applaud it, that "language does not bar us from reality." But he adds as a part of the same sentence, "though reality comes mediated by language."

The problem is, how do we spell out this latter clause in such a way that the former *can* be true? How do we have *mediation* without *modification?* If in his clauses we replace the word "language" with the word "experience" or "consciousness" or even "thought," we find our location in the problematic of modern thought, persisting ever since Descartes "discovered" consciousness. Once you "discover" it you get out only by a miracle. (Descartes of course got out by discovering within his own consciousness an idea, that of a perfect being, of such grandeur that only its object [God] could have caused it. But only his rationalism allowed him to escape the toils of representationalism — a way out no longer available to us, I dare say.)

Quite true to the occasionalist pattern, we find him saying that "the Spirit does not alter biblical meaning." Just as God's mind can move my arm though my mind cannot, so his spirit can bring the true meaning of the text to my mind though my (embodied, culture-bound) mind and body cannot. He is able, as it were, to *bypass* the serpentine routings that my mind on its own must take and that, apparently, *do* invariably alter the biblical meaning if left to themselves.

In language that I like very much Vanhoozer states: "The Spirit progressively disabuses us of those ideological or idolatrous prejudices that prevent us from receiving the message." (Again, this aspect of the Spirit's work too aids understanding in general.) In so doing, the Spirit renders the Word *effective*. To read in the Spirit does not mean to import some new sense to the text, but rather to let the letter be or, better, to apply the letter rightly to one's life. The Spirit of understanding is the efficacy of the Word, its perlocutionary power. According to John Owen, the Spirit is "the primary efficient cause" of our understanding of Scripture. Yet the Spirit's illumining work is not independent of our own efforts to understand. I must *try* to raise my arm or it will not go up! "It is the Spirit's activity, effected through our own labor in exegesis, analysis, and application, of showing us what the text means for us."[2]

2. J. I. Packer, *Keep in Step with the Spirit* (Leicester: Inter-Varsity Press, 1984), p. 239.

Difficulties for occasionalism begin to emerge when we ask the question, Why is it that God's mind can make my arm go up but my mind cannot, since they are both *minds?* The answer seems at bottom to be nothing other than that God can do *anything,* and hence he can make my arm go up. Cannot he who spoke worlds (including my arm) into existence make my arm go up? And cannot this same one cause me to get the right interpretation of a text that he has produced? On pain of blasphemy we can only say: "Yes, surely he can!" But then we must acknowledge that from the fact that he *can* do it does not follow that he *does* do it. And we also must wonder, occasionally, what exactly it is that he does in overriding our culture-bound condition to get the message to us. *How* does he do it?

And, finally, the frightening question: How do we know when (or that) he is doing it? If we say in response that we recognize the presence of the Spirit in people by their confession that Jesus has come in the flesh, is that not circular, in that it is a criterion derived from the New Testament text itself, which we — it is said — can get right only by the aid of the Spirit? Or if we say that the mark of the Spirit in people is their obedience to the commands, promises, warnings, and narratives in the text, is that not also circular, in that it presupposes that we have got the right understanding of the commands, promises, and so forth?

The basic idea seems right, and it is not a wholly new one. In *De Magistro* St. Augustine argued that the understanding of words period required the presence of the Inward Teacher, Christ the Logos, to lead us along; for words as sounds and marks are inherently dumb things at best. But saying exactly how it works, and how we know when it is working, is a daunting task.[3]

One might say, utilizing the language of John Owen quoted above, that God just *causes* us to have the right understanding of the text. No doubt He could do this. But if that is all there is to it, we still might not know we had the right understanding, for we might not know whether in a given case he is causing the interpretation that we have. Also, that would simply dispense with hermeneutical activity as a human undertaking. We are reminded here of preachers who say (usually shout): "I'm not telling you what I think! I'm telling you what God says!" The operant idea here is

---

3. See St. Augustine, *Concerning the Teacher and On the Immortality of the Soul,* ed. Sterling P. Lamprecht, trans. George G. Leckie (New York: Appleton-Century-Crofts, 1938), chaps. 11-12.

that of altogether circumventing human consciousness with its deadly contaminations. But then of course we lose the personal nature of God's relationship to us. We are simply — at least in the moment of inspiration — a keyboard on which God plays, without even our knowledge that it is *he* that is doing the playing. We could only guess.

The only alternative to this model of manipulation from behind the scenes is one where the Spirit "guides" us into the right interpretation through what he places *before* our minds, whether it be burning bushes, angels, audible words, inner images, feelings or thoughts, or the nonphysical "presence" of pure spirits. But of course this means that we will have to be capable of and responsible for the interpretation of what is thus placed before us, and we are back in the fire. Either we can get this right on our own or we cannot. If we cannot, the Spirit must help us. But then . . .

A way out might be along the following lines. We could abandon representationalism as a general theory of human consciousness, and defend a realism in the light of which it does not follow from the fact that I am conscious of something that it appears to me to be what it is not in itself. Does Vanhoozer have something like this in mind with his "realism principle"? This is, of course, basic philosophical work, and the conclusion is contrary to nearly every prominent contemporary writer in the philosophy of mind and language, as well as in epistemology.

Then we might do painstaking phenomenological work on putative experiences of the divine Word and presence, moving toward a systematic description and analysis of the various kinds of experiences involved and of how the cases of the actual presence of God to us and with us are to be distinguished from cases of absence as well as cases of false presence and false absence. An astonishing amount of this type of work has already been done in the spiritual literature that has been produced by the church through the ages. I have tried to be helpful at a popular, nonscholarly level on these matters with my book, *In Search of Guidance: Developing a Conversational Relationship with God.* We need not achieve infallibility on whether or not the Spirit is moving with a particular interpretation or event or tendency, but only sound judgment, practiced in historical/community contexts. Note that the phenomenology of the Spirit's presence would have to be done in such a way that it did not presuppose that we have the right interpretation of texts. Some would say that this will be impossible, but we should be willing to see whether or not it is so in fact. And I want heartily to second Vanhoozer's stress on practice. The presence of the Spirit will, I think, mainly be known as we *act on* the biblical texts, especially those assigned to Jesus himself. It is by action that we enter the reality of the world that the Bible is about. It is *residing* in Jesus' word that permits us to enter the reality of God's rule and become free from domination by other realities (John 8:31-32; cf. 14:15-16). Similarly, by *acting* on knowledge of electricity we become agents in a world where it has play.

Armed with this knowledge of the experience of God, it may be that we can find a way around the impasse that gives rise to hermeneutical occasionalism. Perhaps we can learn the presence of God in such a way that what he places before our minds, in certain cases, as well as the construal given it, can be known to be from him. Stephen Stell's idea, which Vanhoozer seems to adopt, "that the identity of Jesus Christ is defined not only by the narrative framework of the Gospels 'but also by particular experiences in our current existence,'" might be given a workable form.[4] But there will always be a battle over such possibilities so long as intellectual culture is dominated by the view of consciousness (language) as necessarily distortive of what comes before it as an object. On occasion that view has been based on the presumption that human consciousness as such is sinful. Today, apparently, it is enough that it be consciousness.

Kevin Vanhoozer makes many excellent points that I must leave untouched. His thesis of the primacy of the theological for all understanding is, I think, precisely right, and is of tremendous importance not only in the academic/scholarly context, but in today's political, social, and personal context as well. It is a major part of the redemptive message that the people of Jesus must bring to the current world. But I must leave off with that.

---

4. Stephen L. Stell, "Hermeneutics in the Theology and the Theology of Hermeneutics: Beyond Lindbeck and Tracy," *Journal of the American Academy of Religion* 61 (1993): 695.

Contributors

Ellen T. Charry is assistant professor of systematic theology at the Perkins School of Theology. She is author of *By the Renewing of Your Minds: The Pastoral Function of Christian Doctrine*.

Willie James Jennings is assistant professor of theology and black church studies at the Duke Divinity School. He has published articles and reviews in *Modern Theology*, the *Journal of Black Sacred Music*, and *Pro Ecclesia*.

Roger Lundin is professor of English at Wheaton College. He is the author of *The Culture of Interpretation: Christian Faith and the Postmodern World* and, with Anthony Thiselton and Clarence Walhout, *The Responsibility of Hermeneutics*.

David Lyon is professor of sociology at Queen's University. His publications include *Postmodernity* and *The Electronic Eye: The Rise of the Surveillance Society*.

Donald G. Marshall is professor of English and head of the English department at the University of Illinois at Chicago. He edited *Literature as Philosophy/Philosophy as Literature* and, with Joel Weinsheimer, translated the second revised edition of Hans-Georg Gadamer's *Truth and Method*.

I. Howard Marshall is professor of New Testament at the University of

Aberdeen. His publications include *I Believe in the Historical Jesus* and *The Origins of New Testament Christology*.

Kevin J. Vanhoozer is senior lecturer in theology and religious studies at the University of Edinburgh. He is the author of *Biblical Narrative in the Philosophy of Paul Ricoeur: A Study in Hermeneutics and Theology*.

Merold Westphal is professor of philosophy at Fordham University. His publications include *Suspicion and Faith: The Religious Uses of Modern Atheism* and *Becoming a Self: A Reading of Kierkegaard's "Concluding Unscientific Postscript."*

Dallas Willard is professor of philosophy at the University of Southern California. He is the author of *Logic and the Objectivity of Knowledge: A Study in Husserl's Early Philosophy* and *The Spirit of the Disciplines: Understanding How God Changes Lives*.

Nicholas Wolterstorff is the Noah Porter Professor of Philosophical Theology at Yale University. His most recent books are *John Locke and the Ethics of Belief* and *Divine Discourse: Philosophical Reflections on the Claim that God Speaks*.

Index